BEYOND
BLESSED

BEYOND BLESSED

GOD'S PERFECT PLAN TO OVERCOME
ALL FINANCIAL STRESS

ROBERT MORRIS

WITH A FOREWORD
BY DAVE RAMSEY

Faith Words

NASHVILLE   NEW YORK

FaithWords
Hachette Book Group
1290 Avenue of the Americas, New York, NY 10104
faithwords.com
twitter.com/faithwords

Originally published in hardcover and ebook by FaithWords in January 2019
First Trade Paperback Edition: January 2020

FaithWords is a division of Hachette Book Group, Inc. The FaithWords name and logo are trademarks of Hachette Book Group, Inc.

The publisher is not responsible for websites (or their content) that are not owned by the publisher.

The Hachette Speakers Bureau provides a wide range of authors for speaking events. To find out more, go to www.hachettespeakersbureau.com or call (866) 376-6591.

Unless otherwise noted, Scripture quotations are taken from the New King James Version®. Copyright © 1982 by Thomas Nelson. Used by permission. All rights reserved.

Scripture quotations marked (KJV) are taken from the Holy Bible, King James Version.

Scripture quotations marked (NLT) are taken from the Holy Bible, New Living Translation, copyright © 1996, 2004, 2015 by Tyndale House Foundation. All rights reserved.

Scripture quotations marked (NASB) are taken from the New American Standard Bible®, copyright © 1960, 1962, 1963, 1968, 1971, 1972, 1973, 1975, 1977, 1995 by The Lockman Foundation. Used by permission. www.Lockman.org

Scripture quotations marked (NIV) are taken from the Holy Bible, New International Version®, NIV®. Copyright © 1973, 1978, 1984, 2011 by Biblica, Inc.™ Used by permission of Zondervan. All rights reserved worldwide. www.zondervan.com. The "NIV" and "New International Version" are trademarks registered in the United States Patent and Trademark Office by Biblica, Inc.™

Library of Congress Control Number: 2018953664

ISBNs: 978-1-5460-1009-8 (hardcover), 978-1-5460-1012-8 (ebook),
978-1-5460-1353-2 (signed edition), 978-1-5460-1339-6 (int'l edition, South Africa),
978-1-5460-1008-1 (trade paperback), 978-1-5460-3725-5 (TBN edition)

Printed in the United States of America

LSC-C

Printing 3, 2022

I dedicate this book to my wife Debbie.
Because of you, my life has truly been beyond blessed!

CONTENTS

FOREWORD

by Dave Ramsey

I like to say that I met God on the way up, but I really got to know Him on the way down. That's because I became a believer before my wife, Sharon, and I filed for bankruptcy. But the early days of my walk with God took place inside the crucible of that financial disaster.

And since I have the gift of skepticism, I questioned everything about my new faith—including why my church seemed to go on and on about money. Thankfully, God was really patient with this young man. He taught me that my pastor talked a lot about money because *the Bible* talked a lot about money. He also exposed me to some great Christian thought leaders who shaped my take on God's ways of handling money. I soaked up everything I could find from teachers like Larry Burkett, Ron Blue, and Howard Dayton.

I also crossed paths with a pastor from Texas named Robert Morris.

Over the years, Pastor Robert and I have become close friends. He's spoken to my team at Ramsey Solutions, and I've had the privilege of speaking to his amazing congregation at Gateway Church. Plus, God has used his first book, *The Blessed Life*, to strengthen my understanding of things like giving, generosity, and contentment.

Honestly, I use something that I've learned from Robert Morris almost every day of my life.

And that's why I'm so excited about the book that you're holding.

See, I talk with hurting people on the radio every day. I meet them face-to-face at our live events. I see them at their worst, when they're so scared they can hardly breathe and when their marriages are hanging on by a thread. For them, giving and generosity feel like bucket list items—dreams that might become a reality "one of these days."

Meanwhile, they're just fighting to stay alive. Like so many others, they're living paycheck-to-paycheck, drowning in a sea of student loans, car loans, and credit card debt. They're basically good people. They aren't stingy or rebelling against God. They simply don't have the margin to give.

And that's what makes the message of this book so important.

Pastor Robert compares being wise with money to a person standing on two legs. *The Blessed Life* explained the importance of one leg: generous giving. But *Beyond Blessed* focuses on the other leg: biblical stewardship.

Of the two, giving is the easiest to grasp. But stewardship is just as important.

The Bible clearly teaches that God owns it all. Not just a tenth of your income or an occasional love offering or a pledge to a capital campaign. *Everything* belongs to Him. He owns the cattle on a thousand hills, but He also owns the hills!

What's more, He's given each of us a portion of His stuff to manage wisely. That's really what stewardship is all about. It's letting God be the boss of everything that's in your hands. It's using His blessings His way for His glory.

Now, that's not easy in this world. Our culture swings from one extreme that says wealth is evil to the other extreme that says wealth is a sure sign of God's love. But, as Pastor Robert reminds us, neither is the truth.

Beyond Blessed helps you navigate money, wealth, and generosity from a biblical perspective. It teaches you the tactical things that I love like budgeting and saving and getting out of debt. But it also shows you why all that has to be done with a spirit of contentment and absolute dependence on God.

Simply put, Pastor Robert teaches you how to stand on both legs of wise biblical finances. He shows you how to be a great steward so that you can become an outrageously generous giver.

Over the years, I've been blessed to rub elbows with some awesome leaders. But I've never met anyone who understands biblical stewardship and generous giving better than Robert Morris. Plus, he doesn't just *know* this stuff. He *lives* it every, single day. His example inspires me to reflect Jesus more clearly through my life and my money.

I believe it will inspire you, as well.

START HERE!

I didn't see it coming. How could I? All these years later it still stuns and humbles me as I look at what God did, and continues to do, with that humble little effort.

Way back in 2001, it never occurred to me that a simple response to a request from a dear friend and mentor would set in motion a publishing phenomenon that here, all these years later, would still be spreading around the world touching hearts and impacting lives. In other words, no one is more surprised than I that my first-ever book, a little collection of things God had taught me about generosity, is a perennial best seller among Christian books.

As I write these words, *The Blessed Life* has been reprinted dozens of times in dozens of languages. Millions of tattered, dog-eared copies circulate hand to hand around the world. I'm told that a not-insignificant portion of the book's robust annual sales now comes in the form of bulk orders, as pastors of churches large and small buy one copy for every household in their congregations. Among these pastors are men like Craig Groeschel, pastor of one of America's largest church networks, Life.Church; Max Lucado; Rick Warren; Chris Hodges; Joel Osteen; and Brian Houston.

Please understand I'm not sharing this because I want you to be impressed. On the contrary, as I said at the outset, no one is more startled by that book's success than I am. No, I tell you this for a simple reason. To understand the power, purpose, and potential of the book you currently hold in your hands, you must understand what I intended *The Blessed Life* to impart and, just as importantly, what it was *not* created to teach. Here on the opening pages of this book, it is vital that you understand the remarkable origin story of this book's eldest brother. My firstborn, if you will. Only then will you be able to fully benefit from what is to follow.

Back in 2001 I was a young...okay, youngish...okay, a forty-year-old pastor of a fledgling church startup. We had launched Gateway Church with a few dozen people in a living room about a year and a half earlier, but it had grown rapidly. In fact, we had just moved into a rented facility—a former church now operating as a day-care center. As a result, we were enjoying the wildly extravagant luxury of not having to set up and tear down our sound system and projector every Saturday night. We could just set everything up and leave it! This also enabled us to add Sunday-morning services, whereas we had been limited to one Saturday-night service only in our previous spot.

The move accelerated our growth to the point that we quickly found ourselves ministering to more than five hundred people or more on a weekend. While this seemed like a vast multitude to us at the time, the reality was that Gateway wasn't even one of the largest churches on our street, much less one of the largest in North America. It was in this season that a friend approached me with a surprising request on behalf of James Robison.

In the unlikely event that you're not familiar with James, you need to know he is a truly wonderful man of God who has been used mightily by the Lord over the last five decades to positively impact the lives of people around the world and advance the kingdom of God in a variety of ways. Like me, he began his ministry as an itinerating Baptist evangelist and was used to introduce hundreds of thousands to new life in Jesus Christ.

At the peak of his influence and notoriety in that denominational stream, James had a transformative encounter with the Holy Spirit that set him and his ministry on a new trajectory. For the last twenty-five years, James has ministered to millions via his daily *Life Today* television broadcast, using it to fund humanitarian efforts that have saved and improved countless lives all over the world.

Not long after I surrendered my life to Christ as a nineteen-year-old and sensed a call to full-time ministry, I went to work in the mail room and telephone prayer center of James' ministry, Life Outreach International. Needless to say, he has been a great role model, mentor, and friend to me through the years.

Two decades later, I found myself the pastor of a young, expanding church with James Robison as a member of my congregation. (If you don't think this was a little intimidating, you should try it!) That's when he sent the request that set all this in motion.

James had heard me speak about how to cultivate a heart and lifestyle of generosity—toward God and others. This resonated with him powerfully because he had grown concerned about the prevalence of a "give to get" message being proclaimed from many pulpits and media ministries. That message seemed to suggest that the primary motivation for believers to be generous is the expectation of receiving even more back in return. In contrast, I advocated a "give to live" and "give to love" heart motivation for God's people. In other words, I was teaching our congregation that believers should be the most generous people on earth simply because our hearts are overflowing with gratitude to God for His extravagant, gracious

> Believers should be the most generous people on earth simply because our hearts are overflowing with gratitude to God.

gifts of salvation and eternal life. I taught that we give to God and others for the sheer joy of giving and because God is a giver—therefore, as His children, we should naturally take after our Father. Instead of a "give to get" message, I preach a "get to give" message.

James believed this kind of teaching needed to be exposed to a wider audience, so he presented me with a challenge coupled with an opportunity. If I would expand on these messages in book form, he would offer the book on his television program and have me on to talk about it.

It represented an intriguing challenge. On one hand, I was a more-than-busy pastor of a church virtually exploding with growth. I found myself coming and going several times in a typical week. The thought of finding time to write a whole book—something I'd never done before—seemed impossible. On the other hand, I agreed wholeheartedly with James that the body of Christ needed to get this revelation of generous giving from a higher motivation. More importantly, I sensed that this invitation wasn't ultimately from James Robison. It was God who was opening this door because He wants all of His people to experience the joy that results from being a cheerful, extravagant giver. I felt the Spirit of God prompting me to say yes to this invitation, and to trust Him with the task of actually getting the book written. So I did.

Ultimately, the writing of *The Blessed Life* proved far less painful than I imagined it would be. I've learned through years of walking with God that He always supernaturally empowers us to do what He asks of us, if only we'll step out in faith and trust. I began by slipping away for a long weekend retreat with a pile of scribbled notes and a voice recorder. After some time of prayer and fellowship with God, I organized my notes, turned that recorder on, and began pouring out my heart and thoughts about living a lifestyle of generosity.

The words flowed far more freely than I'd thought possible. Long-forgotten stories and incidents rose up in my memory. I said things I didn't even know I knew! By the time my getaway was over I had hours and hours of teaching on tape. My next step was to have these recordings transcribed. I spent some time refining them, then turned them over to a gifted editor who happened to be a member of Gateway Church and understood at a deep level the truths and principles I wanted to convey. He cleaned up and polished the emerging work further and soon we had a bona fide book manuscript ready for printing. The rest, as they say, is history.

The initial print run of thirty thousand copies was quickly exhausted, so additional printings followed. Soon, major publishing houses started expressing interest in taking *The Blessed Life* on as a published title. I said yes to one of them and soon the book was being sold everywhere!

Now, I was a publishing novice back then. I didn't know enough about it to know what was normal in the Christian book industry. Since then I've learned that most books, if they're successful, experience an initial surge of sales that trails off fairly quickly. But that didn't happen with *The Blessed Life*. It seemed to just keep growing with each passing year—fueled by the word of mouth of those who had been touched and helped by it. In fact, it's still going strong today.

So why a "sequel" all these years later? Well, actually it's really more of a *prequel*, and you'll understand why in a moment.

Two Legs Required

I have a vague childhood memory of seeing a cartoon episode in which a character has one shoe nailed to the floor. He runs as hard as he can but can only spin in circles. It's comical to see a cartoon character in that plight. But there is nothing funny at all about seeing my fellow Christians live that way. Allow me to explain.

Since writing *The Blessed Life*, I've heard countless testimonies from individuals, couples, and families who read it, embraced its message, and experienced wonderful, life-transforming results. They responded to its challenge to cultivate a lifestyle of generosity and started giving joyfully and liberally. Even extravagantly. In doing so they discovered what my wife, Debbie, and I did long ago—namely, that

> You can't outgive God.

you can't outgive God, and that blessing others as the Holy Spirit prompts you is just about the most fun any human being can have. They learned that putting God first in their finances and recognizing that it all belongs to Him anyway results in freedom, peace, and joy in every area of their lives. This indeed *is the blessed life.*

But that's not the only kind of testimony I've heard over the years. Another, less encouraging theme emerged from some who read and tried to follow the book's core message about giving. From time to time I've had someone come up to me on the street or at a conference and say something along the lines of, "I tried it, but it didn't work."

Of course, my usual response was, "Tried what?"

"Giving. My spouse and I started giving as you suggested in your book, but we're still buried in credit card debt."

Initially I was puzzled by these kinds of comments. I wasn't connecting the dots because, in my mind, they were unrelated to what the book was actually about. After all, I didn't write a book called *The Blessed Pocketbook* or *The Blessed Balance Sheet*. I shared spiritual truths and insights for experiencing God's blessing upon your entire existence—which encompasses your health, emotions, relationships, and, yes, your finances.

Gradually I began to understand that I had built the message of *The Blessed Life* on an assumption. If you think of that book's message as a house, then there is an underlying assumption serving as the house's foundation. That foundational assumption is this:

We have to live within our means.

Put another way, *you can't spend (or give) more than you have.* Now, I know there's nothing particularly deep or profound about that statement. It is a concept so simple a child can grasp it. Indeed, I learned this principle from my wise and frugal parents early on in life.

My father was and is one of the most generous men I've ever known. Over the years, I've watched him give thousands of dollars to the kingdom and bless struggling people with cars and even houses! He's made personal loans to young couples for down payments on their first house, to families who were rebounding from financial disasters, to people who had lost their jobs, and to widows who needed reliable transportation. And he still does.

He doesn't make a big deal out of his one-man benevolence banking operation he's been running for decades. On the contrary, his generosity flies under the radar of most of the people who know him. But he did once show me the little black ledger book that contained all of the personal loans that were still outstanding. Quickly totaling them in my head brought me to more than $350,000! One of these was a loan of $20,000 to an older widow who needed a car. My dad had told her to pay whatever she could. She was faithfully repaying him at a rate of $20 per month. My mathematical mind quickly realized the loan would never recover even a fraction of that money. Of course, he wasn't bothered by that. As I flipped through the pages, I realized that most of the loans were like that. I asked my father, "Do you have any collateral for these loans?" He said, "No, just their word." I said, "Well, what if they don't pay you back?" His eyes welled up with tears as he choked the words out: "Well, then... I got to bless them!"

My father is definitely one of the greatest givers I've ever known! Not coincidentally, he is also one of the greatest *stewards* I've ever known, and those two realities are related. Just think about it: How can you generously give to others if you have nothing to give?

Dad is a civil engineer by trade and even owned his own company for many years. I've been told more than once that he is a mathematical genius. Numbers add up in his mind effortlessly. So, if he's going to help someone with a $5,000 loan, and he has payroll and monthly expenses to meet, he has to be able to live on a budget that allows him to meet all of his obligations *and* be extremely generous! My dad certainly modeled wise, frugal, prudent stewardship.

I carried this ethic into my marriage. Debbie and I married young, and I was clueless and foolish about many things at that point in my life. But understanding the basic, unforgiving math of income versus outgo wasn't one of them. I knew you can't spend more than you make. I wasn't earning much money in those days. I suspect that by the government's official definition, we were literally *poor*. Yet we did whatever was necessary to live on less than what I made. And once I fully surrendered my life to Jesus and experienced God's extravagant gift of forgiveness and wholeness, doing so included managing our finances in such a way that we could tithe faithfully and give generously whenever the Spirit nudged us.

I honestly assumed most, if not all, believers understood this. So, I didn't address it in *The Blessed Life*. It seemed obvious to me that being a generous person involved redirecting your discretionary spending money, which in turn required...you know...actually *having* discretionary spending money. Furthermore, wise money management—as important as that topic is—simply wasn't what James Robison asked me to write about. He asked me to explain my biblical approach to giving, one that was and is a sharp contrast to the prevalent "give to get" philosophy.

The fact is, a life of true blessing walks on *two* legs. One of these legs—the focus of my first book—is generosity. It is absolutely necessary to be generous to experience the full measure of God's blessing. However, the vital *first* leg is managing your financial resources wisely and prudently so you'll actually be able to be generous. That is the focus of the book you now hold in your hands. This is why I said that, in a sense, it is as much a prequel as a sequel to *The Blessed Life*. It is also why I was put in remembrance of that cartoon character with one foot nailed to the floor. Trying to be more generous without also becoming a prudent manager of resources (especially money) is like trying to run with one foot nailed to the floor. It will be exhausting, frustrating, and fruitless. This is precisely what I saw in the faces of those people who came up to me saying things like, "Pastor Robert, I've started giving but I'm still trapped in credit card debt."

Here's wonderful news. The ability to wisely manage wealth and material possessions is not a talent with which you're gifted at birth. It's a skill. This means it can be taught and learned. It is a form of wisdom, and the book of Proverbs wouldn't encourage us to "get

> The ability to wisely manage wealth and material possessions is not a talent with which you're gifted at birth. It's a skill.

wisdom" (4:7) if it weren't available to everyone with enough humility to receive it.

There is a biblical word for this skill, but I'm almost reluctant to use it here because it's gotten a bad reputation through misuse and abuse. Too many Christians have a wrong concept of what this word denotes. Here goes, anyway. I'm talking about...*stewardship*!

Many people who have been in church most of their lives have come to associate the word *stewardship* solely with giving to the church. They have been conditioned to view stewardship as just a code word for giving offerings or tithing. This is understandable because this is precisely the context in which it's so often used. If a church has a "stewardship emphasis week," it invariably means a week in which everyone is exhorted to give more generously. A "stewardship campaign" is often the label applied to an initiative to raise funds for a new building. Over time, we've been trained to hear the word *stewardship* and think "giving more." But that's not what I mean when I use that term at Gateway Church—because that's not the way it is used in the Bible.

The fact is that stewardship is simply about being a wise, prudent, and skillful *steward* of all the resources God has placed in your hands. So, what is a steward? We'll explore this question in greater depth in the chapters that follow, but for now let me give you a quick working definition. One of the main definitions for *steward* in the *Oxford English Dictionary* is "a person employed to manage another's property, especially a large house or estate." As used in the Bible, it refers to a person who is left in charge of another person's assets. A steward is entrusted with protecting, maintaining, nurturing, and/or growing things—a business, a farm, a household, or some funds—that belong to someone else.

God made Adam and Eve (and by extension their descendants) stewards of the entire earth. He left it in their care to "tend and keep" (Gen. 2:15) and gave them instructions to maximize its potential, saying, "Be fruitful and multiply; fill the earth and subdue it; have dominion..." (Gen. 1:28). In a similar way, God entrusts many things to each of us. As the Creator of everything, including us, it all belongs to Him. Yet He leaves in our care assets such as time, talents, relationships, and yes, wealth. Handling these precious assets prudently qualifies us for blessing. And for the privilege of being entrusted with more.

Numerous parables of Jesus feature stewards—both good and bad. In the coming chapters, we'll explore these parables and mine them for divine wisdom and insight. For now, just know that on the pages that follow, I will lay out the principles, precepts, and patterns that make you a sound, skillful handler of all God has entrusted to you. We'll focus on wealth, but the principles translate to every resource and asset category.

This will include practical skills such as budgeting, handling debt, and financial planning. In fact, these skills are so vital that our church established an entire ministry we call Gateway Stewardship in order to help our members learn them. As I said, the reality that any believer can learn the practical keys to becoming a wise steward is wonderful news and should give you hope as you begin this journey.

Here is even better news. As with everything else in the Christian life, as you step out in faith and obedience to become a more biblical steward of what God has entrusted to you, He will run to meet you and help you! Supernatural power from heaven is ready and waiting to provide miraculous help to you as you set out to become a wise steward. I know this

> As you step out in faith and obedience to become a more biblical steward of what God has entrusted to you, He will run to meet you and help you!

to be true because Debbie and I have experienced it time and again. But we're not special or unusual. On the pages that follow, you will encounter dozens of real-life testimonies of regular believers just like you who desired to align their financial lives with the Bible's wisdom. (I've changed or omitted their names to protect their privacy, but their stories are very real.) Unfailingly, they found they weren't alone in their quest to become better stewards. As they stepped out, they discovered a mighty heavenly wind at their backs, accelerating their progress as God honored their decision to do things His way.

Please get this: God blesses, helps, and rewards your heartfelt efforts to be a better steward.

I wrote this book as a companion to *The Blessed Life* because God wants to bless you. It's His nature and desire to do so. But it's hard for Him if you're not both a wise steward *and* a generous giver. Indeed, the first enables the second. Generosity is the goal. Wise stewardship is the vital means to achieving that goal.

Yes, the blessed life travels on two legs. I'm here now to help you get that first, vital leg in place and working strong. Then and only then will you be free to be a generous, joyous giver. And with those two legs in place in your life, they'll take you to a place "beyond blessed."

CHAPTER ONE

MAXIMUM IMPACT, MINIMUM STRESS

I want to invite you to daydream a bit. No, I'm not suggesting that you mentally check out and head to the golf course or the beach in your imagination. I'm asking you to pause a moment and picture, as vividly and with as much detail as you can, how it would feel to live without financial pressure.

Imagine that you always have money left at the end of the month, rather than too much month left at the end of your money. I'm talking about a life in which you've forgotten what it feels like to have worry or stress about your finances. When confronted with a purchasing decision, your first thought is, "Lord, *should* I buy this?" rather than, "How can I afford this?" Imagine a life of daily peace, laying your head on your pillow at night with a satisfied soul, and sleeping like a baby. If you're married, you and your spouse routinely pray about spending priorities but never fight about money.

Picture a life in which you get to bless others whenever and wherever the Spirit moves you. This is a life turbocharged with energy, purpose, and fulfillment because you get to consistently invest in the people and causes that mean the most to you. In this imagined existence, you live with the assurance that you are, in the words of Jesus, laying up treasure in heaven (Matt. 6:19–21). But in the meantime, you're having a ball here on earth. How fun this life is!

The highlight of a typical day might be noticing the frazzled-looking young mother in the grocery store aisle comparing prices on the cheapest brands of peanut butter while using her phone as a calculator and fighting back tears. You approach her, hand her a fifty-dollar bill, quietly say that God wants her to know that He sees her and cares about her, and simply walk away. Indeed, you spend your days looking for opportunities to be an answer to some desperate person's whispered prayer—routinely having the privilege of serving as a living, breathing, tangible manifestation of God's love for them.

Imagine not getting a sudden pit in your stomach when you think about your retirement years or old age. Like the wise, prudent woman of Proverbs 31, you smile at the future (v. 25).

Go ahead and imagine all of this, and any other aspects that come to mind of a life free from money pressure. As sharply and vividly as you can, picture yourself, your family, your home, your career in snapshots and video images of how it could be. Picture being free to follow to the fullest the adventure God wants to live alongside you.

> See yourself experiencing a life of maximum impact and minimum financial stress.

See yourself experiencing a life of maximum impact and minimum financial stress.

Well, what do you think? Does that kind of life seem appealing? Gratifying? Peaceful? Of course it does. However, I don't want you to get the wrong idea. What you just envisioned was *not* necessarily the life of a wealthy person. In fact, many extremely wealthy people spend as much or more time worrying, fighting, obsessing, and stressing about money as anyone. The rich are more likely to be on antidepressants or antianxiety medications than average working-class folks. Millionaires and billionaires commit suicide with shocking regularity.

Nor did I just encourage you to fantasize about winning the lottery. A 2016 article in *Time* magazine pointed out that many people who win giant jackpots "wind up unhappy or wind up broke."[1] As an expert cited in that article pointed out, "About 70 percent of people who suddenly receive a windfall of cash will lose it within a few years."[2] A 2013 article in *Forbes* titled "Why Lottery Winners Crash After a Big Win"[3] cited a study of Florida lottery winners that found that more than 5 percent of them were in bankruptcy only five years out from their big "win." The author interviewed numerous jackpot winners and found a startling number of them miserable and alienated from everyone they cared about. One woman referred to the money she and her husband had won as "a curse."[4] Another study revealed that "sudden wealth" didn't take pressure off marriages, either. In fact, it actually increased the likelihood of divorce for married couples.[5]

The wonderful fact is that the truly "blessed life" you just envisioned is available to everyone, regardless of income bracket or social status. You can have that life. Anyone can. It requires only one thing: consistently living within your means. That's the truth. Of course, just because it's *simple* doesn't mean it's easy or comes naturally. If living within your means were easy, it wouldn't be such a rare thing in our culture. (By the way, it wasn't rare a few generations ago. In fact, it was the norm. We've lost a vital virtue somewhere along the way.)

Wherever you stand right now, however ill equipped you may feel, however overwhelming your challenges may seem, you can take the first crucial steps today—then follow through all the way to a life "beyond blessed."

It's not too late. You haven't gone too far to course correct. You are not disqualified in any way because of anything you've done, haven't done, or suffered. You don't need to have any specific talent or aptitude. You don't have to come with anything more than a surrendered, humble heart and a willingness to embrace biblical wisdom. And you can start right now. (In fact, by picking up this book, you've already started!)

I know this, not because I know *you*, but because I've seen the precepts and practices I'm about to present to you work for an astonishing variety of people from every imaginable starting point. I've received thousands of letters from readers whose lives were changed by *The Blessed Life*, but one special letter touched me in a particularly meaningful way.

It came from a lady who received the book when she was a nonbeliever in the midst of a divorce. She read it and God used it to transform her life on multiple levels. She got a glimpse of the reality that God is good and that He loves her, so she gave her life to Christ. She promptly asked her soon-to-be ex-husband to read it, too. He did so, and although it was never envisioned to be an evangelistic book, he got saved as well. As a result, their marriage was saved. And their lives radically changed as they started putting God first in their lives.

But that's just the "backstory" she shared in her letter. This woman continued by describing a visit to Gateway Church. Eager to share her excitement, she told her story to the first person she met: our receptionist, who was alone in the church lobby, except for a nearby janitor taking out the trash just within earshot of the conversation. After finishing her story of how *The Blessed Life* had impacted her life, she asked where she could find the church bookstore. She hoped to buy ten copies for her friends and family. The receptionist directed her around the corner to our bookstore. When this woman arrived there a few minutes later, she found ten copies already set out and waiting for her. She asked how much they would cost—unsure how many she could afford—and the clerk smiled and said, "Not a thing. They're yours! The price has been paid!"

Startled, the visitor asked our checkout helper to repeat herself. "Someone paid for the books. They're yours to take. Have a blessed day!" The woman remained confused and pressed our store clerk for clarification. The bookstore helper leaned in and smiled. "When you spoke to the receptionist," she said, "did you happen to see the young man working behind you?" The visitor barely remembered.

"Do you mean the janitor taking out the trash?"

"Yes. He must have heard your story," the helper continued, "because he ran down here and bought these books for you."

The visitor couldn't believe it. Overcome with gratitude and wonder, she gathered up two shopping bags filled with *The Blessed Life* and prepared to leave. As she did, the desk helper offered one last tidbit of information about the blessing: "Oh, by the way. That janitor is Pastor Robert's son."

Yes, that was my son James, who was a student working part-time in our church facility maintenance department back then. It was he who overheard the lady's testimony and hurried down the hall for the privilege of blessing her, assuming he would remain anonymous. I don't share this story solely because I'm a proud dad, although you'd better believe it blessed me immensely to read that letter. I share it to encourage you that when a mom and dad start down the path of living wisely in order to live generously, their lives aren't the only ones changed. Younger eyes are watching, learning far more from what you *do* than from what you say. You see, one of the many benefits of living the blessed life is establishing a legacy. Watching your children become adults who know how to be wise stewards and who understand the joy of generosity is one of the most gratifying things you can experience as a parent.

By the way, today James now leads Gateway Church's stewardship department where he and a team offer financial training to those who request it. They share the very principles and processes I'm about to lay out for you.

My hope now is to help you get there, too—not only so you can experience a life of maximum impact, but also so you can model it for the most important people in your life. Yes, I know these precepts will help you. I've had a front-row seat to watching them work in the lives of my children as they've grown to adulthood and launched households of their own.

Let me paraphrase something Henry David Thoreau once wrote: If you've built a castle in the air, that's okay—just put a foundation under it. The castle of that life

> If you've built a castle in the air, that's okay—just put a foundation under it.

without financial pressure we imagined together a moment ago may seem like it's hovering just beyond your reach—so let's build a foundation under it. That foundation is stewardship. Of course, establishing a foundation requires some effort. So, let's get started on building your life beyond blessed.

Settle the Ownership Issue

So, where does this process start? you ask. How do I begin the journey toward being a wise, faithful steward?

To build a foundation for your new life of maximized impact, we're going to have to dig down into the very bedrock of how we understand God and His ways. That means burrowing down to a couple of simple but fundamental questions.

Whose am I? Or put another way, *To whom do I belong?*

If you're truly born again, the answer is easy.

I belong to God, of course!

That's the right answer. After all, most of us have heard and read the words of I Corinthians 6:19–20 many times: "Or do you not know...you are not your own? For you were bought at a price." Saying yes to Jesus and following Him means laying down our lives and completely surrendering everything to Him. As Jesus once told His disciples, "Whoever seeks to save his life will lose it, and whoever loses his life will preserve it" (Luke 17:33).

Of course, we get the far better end of that deal. In the great exchange at the cross, we get rid of a broken, sin-marred, guilt-soaked life and an eternal future in hell. In return we get wholeness, peace, a cleansed conscience, meaning, and purpose in this life and eternity in heaven, to boot!

There is a broader principle embedded in Jesus' warning: namely, that we invariably lose the things that we—out of selfishness, insecurity, or greed—try to cling to. But the things we release to Him in trust and love invariably come back to us many times over.

Once we settle the issue that we belong to God, there is a related ownership question we must settle in our hearts and minds. It's one thing to acknowledge that you belong to God. But what about all the stuff? Who owns this world and all it contains? Or to bring that question down to a more personal level, *Who owns your stuff?* Who owns the money, home, cars, furniture, electronics, clothes, and all the material goods you routinely, casually call "mine"?

The answer to this question represents the foundational, fundamental, bedrock issue of successful stewardship, and therefore of living a blessed life. There is no path to real blessing that doesn't begin with getting this question settled fully and deeply in our hearts—once and for all time. This question, too, seems to have an obvious answer. Of course God owns it all. In another familiar Scripture, the Word plainly declares,

> The earth is the LORD's, and everything in it.
> The world and all its people belong to him. (Psalm 24:1 NLT)

That's pretty clear, don't you think? Yet God Himself gets even more direct and specific when, out of His own mouth, we hear,

> For all the animals of the forest are mine,
> and I own the cattle on a thousand hills.
> I know every bird on the mountains,
> and all the animals of the field are mine.
> If I were hungry, I would not tell you,
> for all the world is mine and everything in it.
>
> (Psalm 50:10–12 NLT)

God says to you, me, and all humankind, "Do you see that pride of lions over there? Mine. See that herd of cattle? Mine. Do you know how many birds there are on those hills over there? No? Well, I do. If I had a craving for fried chicken, I wouldn't need to ask anyone's permission or notify anyone before picking out a plump fryer. The world and all it contains are legally mine because I made them."

If you have a diamond ring, that diamond came from God's coal and was formed under tremendous pressure in the heart of God's earth. If you're wearing pearls, they came from God's oysters. The paper money in your pocket came from one of God's trees. And the metal formed to construct the car you drive? The wood and stone that form your house? There isn't anything in your life that didn't come from God's creation.

Of course, God isn't greedy. On the contrary, He is extravagantly generous. He is the author and source of agape love, the kind of love that gives sacrificially. It is His greatest joy to bestow gifts and bless. This is His nature.

> It is God's greatest joy to bestow gifts and bless.

This stands in sharp contrast to the fallen nature you and I were born with. It seems that one of the first words any infant learns to say—right after *da-da*—is "Mine!" If you've had children, you know this is true. In fact, they can display it before they can even say it. *Mine!* We're all born with a broken, fearful, grasping spirit. A dread of not having enough. Or running out. Or, heaven forbid, someone else having more.

So, the most fundamental question every believer must answer is, Whose declaration of "mine" is valid—yours or God's? They can't both be valid.

The first question we asked and answered should settle this one. *To whom do I belong?* Because if I belong to God, then there is no question that everything I possess is ultimately His. The logic is inescapable. If God owns you, then *you* don't own you. Again, in the words of Paul,

> Don't you realize that your body is the temple of the Holy Spirit, who lives in you and was given to you by God? You do not belong to yourself, for God bought you with a high price. So you must honor God with your body. (I Corinthians 6:19–20 NLT)

Paul makes clear here that if we're born again, we should view our very bodies as being on loan from God. It's yours to live in as a caretaker for eighty to a hundred years, but it's God's house your spirit is occupying.

Yes, it all belongs to God. Early on in my walk with God I settled this question definitively in my heart, and maybe that is why I struggled less with this stewardship issue than some believers clearly do. Understanding that God *owns* and we *steward* is the most vital understanding you must embrace to begin this journey. A fancier word for "understanding" is *paradigm*. Moving from a "this is all my stuff" way of viewing the world to one of "it's all God's stuff" requires a paradigm shift. We'll dive much deeper into the implications of this paradigm, and how it transforms your approach to, and attitude about, literally everything in the chapters to come. But for now, just understand and embrace this foundational truth. *You are not an owner.* You're a steward of many things entrusted to your care by a loving, generous God. This, of course, leads us to another question:

If I am a steward, what kind of steward am I?

Burdens vs. Blessings

The life of a wise steward is a good life. A happy life. A blessed life.

As your daydream exercise at the opening of this chapter suggested, it is a life free of the grinding, soul-crushing pressure of worry about money, debt, or lack. A life largely without fear of the unexpected.

How rare this is in our day! A 2014 survey of 3,068 adults by the Harris Poll research firm revealed that 72 percent of Americans reported feeling stressed about money at least some of the time during the past month.[6] Twenty-two percent said they experienced *extreme stress* about money during the previous month. A few years ago, a banking organization's study revealed that 76 percent of America's households are living paycheck to paycheck. Half of us have saved up less than a three-month cushion of living expenses. Nearly a quarter of all Americans have no savings at all. A stunning number of us are one or two missed paychecks away from a full-on crisis.[7]

However, the costs of unwise stewardship extend far beyond just the realm of our finances. Long-term financial stress, it turns out, can seriously affect your health. It's been linked to migraines, cardiovascular diseases, work absenteeism, insomnia, and mental health problems including depression and other mood disorders. It raises your risk of metabolic syndrome and diabetes. It can predispose you to unhealthy addictive behaviors as you try to "self-medicate" to feel relief from the pain of stress. All that destruction and misery resulting from an entirely preventable problem.

Tragically, these statistics don't distinguish between followers of Christ and everyone else. And in my experience as a pastor, believers are just as likely to be suffering in these ways. That means this epidemic is swallowing up an incredible amount of money, time, and emotional energy that could have been directed at advancing the work of God's kingdom.

All of this unhappiness and suffering is rooted in poor stewardship, which in turn is rooted ultimately in a failure to recognize that all we have belongs to God. And when you don't know in your deepest knower that you and everything you have really is the Lord's, it's very hard to put Him first in our lives. Now, there's an Old Testament term for having something other than God first in your life. *Idolatry.* This isn't just an Old Testament issue, though. The apostle John closed his first letter to believers with these words:

> Little children, keep yourselves from idols. Amen. (1 John 5:21 KJV)

If putting God first in our finances produces so many benefits, why is this so hard to do? Why is it such a battle to loosen our white-knuckle grip on our money and hold it with an open hand instead? Why do we resist so fiercely God's kind, benevolent, for-our-own-good instructions about tithes, offerings, generosity, and submission to Him in our spending decisions? I believe the answer is twofold:

1. Fear
2. A scarcity mentality

When we don't have a revelation of God's faithfulness and love, we feel personally and solely responsible to be on the lookout for danger and threats. When we don't understand that God is the Creator who brings supernatural multiplication, increase, and abundance, it's easy to live with a constant assumption that whatever little bit we have is all there really is.

In dramatic contrast, putting God first and recognizing that it all belongs to Him liberates us from fear of loss and insufficiency. Think about it. When you own a home, the repairs and upkeep are solely your responsibility. But when you are a tenant, the ultimate responsibility for the property lies with the landlord. Homeowners may lie awake at night worrying about whether the roof needs to be replaced, but tenants never do. If there is a potential problem, they simply pick up the phone and say, "Hey, I think you may have a problem with your roof! You might want to check it out."

> Putting God first and recognizing that it all belongs to Him liberates us from fear of loss and insufficiency.

In a very real sense, this is the daily reality with the steward of God's possessions. This is why replacing your ownership mind-set with the stewardship paradigm is so freeing. This extends far beyond mere money to everything under your control, including your children.

I recall hearing the testimony of a woman who attended our series of stewardship classes at Gateway. This sweet woman was married with three children. As she tells it, from the day she gave birth to her first child, she found herself consumed with fear for the child's safety and well-being. These fears only multiplied as additional little ones were added to their family. She worried obsessively about their safety. As a result, she was reluctant to let them do any of the things most children normally do. Activities, sports, school trips, and even playing outside with friends all filled her with a sense of dread.

She shared that this constant worry and stress was taking a toll on her health. She was having breathing trouble and often couldn't sleep at night. It was also impacting her marriage as well. In the midst of all this, she and her husband decided to attend our stewardship classes led by my son James.

The first session covers a lot of the same ground that we have examined in this chapter—particularly the truth that God is the true owner and we are simply stewards of His stuff. James also points out that God's ownership extends to everything in our care, including our own bodies and our children. At the end of each of these sessions, James leads the class in a time of quiet, prayerful introspection. Participants are encouraged to ask God what He is saying to them through the teaching they just heard.

In those few moments of quietness, God put a loving spotlight on that dear woman's constant, debilitating fears concerning her children. She heard Him gently but emphatically say that she doesn't own her kids; He does. "I created them and entrusted them to you as my steward," she heard the Lord say. "But ultimately it is My job to protect and provide for them. Don't you agree that I'm in a much better position to watch over them than you will ever be? Rest!"

She told us she surrendered her kids to God that night, and for the first time since the birth of her first child, she slept soundly and peacefully. She says she realized that if she wanted what is good for her children, how much more does a good and faithful God want the same thing? After all, she realized, this is the same God who, in love, gave up His only beloved Son so she and her children could experience eternal life.

A simple paradigm shift—from ownership to stewardship—transformed her life and radically changed the atmosphere in her home. This is her testimony. It can be your testimony, too.

When you truly, deep down acknowledge that it's all God's

anyway, you'll feel your spiritual fingers loosen their iron grip on *things*. You'll finally experience release from the crushing burden of thinking you have to hoard everything that comes your way.

It's not ultimately up to you. You can let go now.

Once you do, you'll experience new dimensions in your relationship with God as you rest in His faithfulness. And, having released ownership of yourself and your possessions, you can stand back and watch God work the miracles you've heard about. You can experience the unbelievable provision and intervention about which others testify. When you concede the ownership of all you are, and all you do, and all you own to Him, you reorient yourself into a proper alignment with spiritual reality. Areas of your life you never knew were out of kilter will shift into place. Parts of your walk with God, including your prayer life, your sense of His presence, your passion in worship, will be enhanced by the sudden yielding of contested territory to God.

When you return to God what's already His, you lock down a conviction, deep inside you, that God is absolutely, definitely, 100 percent real and active in your life. Your faith in Him suddenly has, as the expression goes, "skin in the game." You've now put your money where your heart is.

This is the foundation of becoming a good steward. This is who you want to be because the hard, harsh truth is that God cannot bless a bad steward. His goodness and love prevent it. His blessings upon a poor steward will destroy the person and inflict damage to others. Wise stewards, on the other hand, find all of heaven's power and resources deployed to help them.

Are you ready to build upon that foundation? The first element was spiritual in nature. The next one is immensely practical. Let's go.

CHAPTER TWO

MORE THAN A BUDGET

It was a very odd feeling. It just didn't feel exactly... *right* somehow. Turning the key, unlocking the door, and stepping across the threshold into someone else's home when they weren't there felt a little like trespassing, if not outright breaking and entering. Debbie and I walked through the living room and saw framed pictures of someone else's kids and grandkids smiling from the end table and mantel. As we turned on a few lights, I half expected to hear someone shout, "Hey, what do you think you're doing?"

In my head, I knew it was okay for us to be there. We were invited guests. Some good friends had given us use of a vacation home they owned so we wouldn't have to stay in a hotel while on a ministry trip. They were thrilled to give us use of it and had taken great pleasure in giving us the keys, telling us where everything was, and warmly encouraging us to make ourselves at home.

It was certainly a blessing to be there. And without a doubt, we were far more comfortable than we would have been in a cramped hotel room. But despite our hosts' gracious encouragement, there was no way I was going to feel completely "at home." I was careful with everything I touched. I took extra care to avoid making a mess and cleaned up after myself meticulously. (Debbie noticed! She probably wondered, "Where is that guy at *our* house?") I practically tiptoed around the place.

Why? Because I was superconscious that I was a guest there. I never for a moment forgot that the home didn't belong to me. Now, to anyone looking in on us from the outside, it would have looked like we owned the place. We sat in the chairs, prepared food in the kitchen, and slept in the bed. Yet we recognized that it belonged to someone else. We knew we had been entrusted with something valuable that was the property of another family. I was grateful for the use of it, was helped and blessed by it, and thoroughly enjoyed it. Yet I also felt a strong sense of obligation to treat it with respect and care.

Of course, what felt like an oddity all those years ago is now commonplace. In fact, it has become a gigantic global business model. The businesses go by names like Airbnb and HomeAway and VRBO. We live in a day in which it is increasingly common for people to open their homes up to strangers or turn it over entirely. Yet there is still a basic expectation that if you rent it, you'll treat it better than you might if you owned it. If you don't, you'll likely get a bad online rating from the owners and find it difficult to avail yourself of properties in that network in the future. In other words, good renters find their options increasing because of a good reputation among owners. Bad renters get their options narrowed. Really bad renters lose them altogether.

This is the essence of *stewardship*. In the most fundamental sense, stewardship is living life with a heart recognition that your money, your possessions—even your body—do not belong to you. And as I

> Stewardship is living life with a heart recognition that your money, your possessions—even your body—do not belong to you.

pointed out in the previous chapter, wise, diligent stewardship is the key to living a life beyond blessed. I also pointed out that many people wrongly think stewardship is synonymous with giving. Others mistakenly think being a good steward means little more than trying to live on a budget. Now, don't misunderstand—budgeting is very important. It's so important, in fact, that I'll bring you some practical keys to doing it well in a later chapter. But truly wise stewardship involves so much more than just following a budget. For now, just embrace the truth that good stewardship is the path to experiencing the full measure of God's blessings, freedom, and purpose in your life.

Quite simply, you can't expect God to shower you with more resources if you're still mismanaging the ones He's already given you. This can sound harsh, but it is actually God's mercy in action. There are many believers that God simply cannot bless with great wealth because He knows it would destroy them. Few people understand that abundance is a far tougher test of character than poverty.

How do we know that God looks for faithful stewardship before bestowing more resources? This truth is at the heart of one of Jesus' longest and most detailed parables.

A Sobering Parable

If we're seeking God's view of stewardship, a logical place to start is the twenty-fifth chapter of Matthew. There we find Jesus giving His disciples a vivid illustration about how God's kingdom operates.

Jesus filled this story with fascinating detail, so let's look at it in its entirety before we begin mining it for nuggets of insight:

For the kingdom of heaven is like a man traveling to a far country, who called his own servants and delivered his goods to them. And to one he gave five talents, to another two, and to another one, to each according to his own ability; and immediately he went on a journey. Then he who had received the five talents went and traded with them, and made another five talents. And likewise he who had received two gained two more also. But he who had received one went and dug in the ground, and hid his lord's money. After a long time the lord of those servants came and settled accounts with them.

So he who had received five talents came and brought five other talents, saying, "Lord, you delivered to me five talents; look, I have gained five more talents besides them." His lord said to him, "Well done, good and faithful servant; you were faithful over a few things, I will make you ruler over many things. Enter into the joy of your lord." He also who had received two talents came and said, "Lord, you delivered to me two talents; look, I have gained two more talents. besides them." His lord said to him, "Well done, good and faithful servant; you have been faithful over a few things, I will make you ruler over many things. Enter into the joy of your lord."

Then he who had received the one talent came and said, "Lord, I knew you to be a hard man, reaping where you have not sown, and gathering where you have not scattered seed. And I was afraid, and went and hid your talent in the ground. Look, there you have what is yours."

But his lord answered and said to him, "You wicked and lazy servant, you knew that I reap where I have not sown, and gather where I have not scattered seed. So you ought to have deposited my money with the bankers, and at my coming I would have received back my own with interest. Therefore take the talent from him, and give it to him who has ten talents.

"For to everyone who has, more will be given, and he will have abundance; but from him who does not have, even what he has will be taken away. And cast the unprofitable servant into the outer darkness. There will be weeping and gnashing of teeth." (Matthew 25:14–30)

Now, you may have noticed that the words *steward* or *stewardship* didn't appear in Jesus' parable. Yet the concept runs through it from beginning to end. You'll recall that one of the *Oxford English Dictionary*'s definitions of *steward* is "a person employed to manage another's property." In this case, the property owner chose three servants and entrusted each of them with a sum of money to manage while he was away in a "far country." This wasn't a gift. The money did not become theirs when he handed it over. As the parable makes clear, the money never stopped being the property of the original owner. And not only did he expect to get every bit of it back when he returned "after a long time," but he also expected increase on each "talent" he entrusted to these men. This is the very definition of stewardship.

Let's begin by understanding what a "talent" represented in Jesus' time. (Hint: It isn't the ability to play the piano or paint!) No, a talent was a measure of weight, usually used in the Roman era to designate a large, specific quantity of silver, but sometimes of gold.

A talent was equivalent to ten thousand silver denarii, and one silver denarius was one day's wage for a laborer. Now, if you do the math on that and assume a six-day workweek and no vacation weeks, one talent of silver is what a laborer would earn in roughly thirty-two years of working. The takeaway here is that these were large sums of money the master was placing in the care of these servants.

The next thing we notice is that he didn't entrust the same amount to each servant. One was entrusted with five talents of silver, one received two talents, and the other, only one. A modern observer in our politically correct times might take note of this discrepancy and cry "Unfair!" "Preferential treatment!" "Playing favorites!" But we don't have to wonder why the master chose to do this; Jesus explains why right there in His story. The master gave "to each according to his own ability" (v. 15). In other words, these three stewards already had a track record of how skillfully they'd handled and cared for the things the master entrusted to them previously. And the amount they were given to administrate was determined by the master's perception of how much they were able to handle. In other words, a history of how they had managed smaller amounts and simpler things in the past drove the master's confidence in their ability to successfully manage more. There is a key piece of insight there for you and me. Perhaps the reason you haven't been given more is that God knows you can't yet handle it.

> Perhaps the reason you haven't been given more is that God knows you can't yet handle it.

This is precisely why this book is so very important for your future. I'm giving you biblical and practical keys to becoming a wiser, more skillful handler of the Master's things. As you do, you will be entrusted with more. Faithful stewards always are.

Please note that every one of the stewards in Jesus' parable was entrusted with some of the master's resources. That carries an implication for you today...

You Are Already a Steward

You don't decide to become a steward. You already are one. God has entrusted you with a wealth of precious resources—whether you've recognized or embraced the role or not. As we've already seen, everything we have actually belongs to God. The only unanswered question is, What *kind* of steward are you? The goal is to be a good one.

You may not consider yourself wealthy right now, although if you're living in the United States, you're almost certainly rich by global standards. The point is you have some material wealth. Also remember that you're a steward of far more than money or material possessions. God has, at minimum, entrusted you with a "starter package" of nonmonetary gifts whose value exceeds all the material value in the world. He's entrusted you with a priceless soul, with a remarkably created human body, and a given number of precious days in which to use them—otherwise known as *a life*—and with distinctive talents and gifts and a remarkably powerful mind.

Notice that some of the things God has placed in your hands are *external* things like money, possessions, and relationships. But many of them are inside you—your soul, your body, your mind. In the most overlooked example, He's made you a bearer of His image. That means you're created in His holy likeness, and you carry that sacred imprint with you every single moment, like a royal standard held high in battle.

Think about that for a moment. If you've been born again, God actually entrusted you with the likeness of Himself, living inside you. He did this through the most amazing act you could ever imagine—stooping down to exist as one of us, then dying to pay for our own rebellion. By His Holy Spirit, He breathed His breath of life into your dead and dying spirit, making you spiritually alive in Him. What an extraordinary privilege! But that honor is also a responsibility.

In more ways than you could ever imagine, you are a caretaker of His property. That makes you a *steward*. And that brings us back to the key question, What kind of a steward are you? A good one or a bad one? A faithful or a faithless one? Wise or foolish?

Stewards Protect and Expand

Many people evaluate the quality of their stewardship based solely on their budgeting discipline and debt levels. It's certainly true that good stewards live on a budget and are prudent in their use of debt. But being a wise steward of a great king actually means bringing increase to that ruler's kingdom, just as the five-talent steward in Jesus' parable did. You see, when it's all said and done, and we're giving an account of how we lived our lives, it ultimately won't be about money. It will be about souls. It will be about lives impacted. Money matters because poor stewards of all God has entrusted to them don't bring increase to their Lord's kingdom.

On the eve of sending the Israelite tribes into the land of prom-ise to take possession of it, Moses told the people, "And you shall remember the LORD your God, for it is He who gives you power to get wealth, that He may establish His covenant which He swore to your fathers, as it is this day" (Deut. 8:18). The same is true for you and me today. God gives power to get wealth that He may establish His New Covenant of salvation in Jesus Christ. Wealth is for bring- ing souls into His New Covenant kingdom.

You can't be generous with your church or missionary organizations, or Christian humanitarian groups, or your hurting neighbor if you're drowning in debt and living paycheck to paycheck. At the same time, poor stewardship of your time, gifts, and relationships will limit your kingdom impact and influence as well.

Good stewards protect and expand the resources of another. This is precisely why we place money in banks. A bank can only succeed if it earns and keeps your trust to (1) keep your deposits safe and (2) reliably grow them. As a wise saver you may have deposits in several different banks. But if one bank undermines your trust, you may very well divert additional deposits to the bank that has validated your trust.

In a very real sense you and I are God's banks. He puts things (and people) on deposit with us, with the twofold expectation that those things (and people) will be kept safe and will grow. We'll be talking a lot about money as we move forward, but let me stop for a moment and ask you to consider the reality that God has given you *people* to steward as well—particularly if you're a parent or an employer.

Stewards of People

Yes, God entrusts people to you. That also means that at several points in your life, *you* were entrusted to someone else as a stewardship responsibility. Your parents or adult guardians stewarded you for many years. At key points in your life, teachers, coaches, mentors, and employers stewarded you as well. Hopefully all the people to whom you were entrusted were excellent stewards of...*you*! However, it's very likely that some of them weren't. Many of us, at some point in our lives, have fallen under the authority of a bad steward.

When I was a young newlywed, I briefly worked as a traveling assistant for a man—an evangelist—who proved to be a very poor steward of me and my family. I felt a call to ministry and had, in a sense, apprenticed myself to this man so I could learn and grow.

After one typical week of nonstop travel with him, I was missing my sweet wife desperately and she was equally excited about getting a couple of days with me after being alone all week. Just as we arrived home late on Friday night, he casually said, "Hey, by the way, I want you to wax my airplane this weekend. Do a good job." And then he jumped in his car and drove off.

I was stunned and dreaded having to tell Debbie upon my arrival home that evening that we wouldn't be spending much time together over the weekend. As I anticipated, she was very unhappy about it. She believed (correctly, by the way) that it was wrong for this man to deprive us of the time we needed to keep our relationship strong, given the fact that the job tended to keep me away from home all week. In fact, she encouraged me to quit. I understood her feelings, but I didn't feel that God had yet released me to do that.

So, early Saturday morning, I dutifully showed up and began waxing this gentleman's airplane. It took all day Saturday, into the evening, and most of the day on Sunday. These were two precious days that could have—and should have—been spent reconnecting with my young wife. To add insult to injury, on Monday the gentleman laughingly told me, "Oh, by the way, the airplane didn't really *need* to be waxed. I just had you do that to build your character."

Inwardly, all my spiritual alarm bells went off when he said this. I knew this wasn't the way God wanted any organization to be run—least of all a ministry. And although I didn't frame it in these terms at the time, I knew this man was being a bad steward of me. I had placed myself (and by extension my family) in his hands. He was a bank and I was a deposit. In God's eyes, he was responsible and accountable for both my protection and my growth. But in his unwise hands, I was neither safe nor growing. Sadly, he ultimately ended up losing his own family. His marriage fell apart and his relationships with his children became toxic. In the end, he wasn't any better a steward of his family than he was of mine.

If you've been in the hands of an unwise steward, I'm sorry. That's painful. Especially when that bad steward is a father or mother. But it's possible to break that cycle. You can use that painful insight as fuel to drive your purpose to be a wise steward of the lives that have been placed in your care.

> You can use pain as fuel to drive your purpose to be a wise steward of the lives that have been placed in your care.

Remember, in the end, it all belongs to God. As Jesus said in regard to another of His parables about money, "And if you have not been faithful in that which is another's, who will give you that which is your own?" (Luke 16:12). Maybe you want to have your own business one day. Or a profitable side business that turns a hobby or passion into another income stream. Maybe you want to be a leader one day. Or perhaps you simply want to be promoted. Wise stewardship is your pathway to all these good things. God cannot promote poor stewards. If you can't handle zero employees, you can't handle one. If you can't handle one, you certainly can't handle one hundred.

It is the one who is faithful with a little who is ultimately entrusted with more. This is just as true of people as it is of money and possessions.

Settling Accounts

Make no mistake, for all stewards a day of accounting ultimately arrives. Remember, in Jesus' parable the master was gone "a long time"...

> After a long time the lord of those servants came *and settled accounts with them.* (Matthew 25:19, emphasis added)

I'm sure the stewards in Jesus' parable would have been tempted to wonder if perhaps the master wasn't coming back at all. It would have been easy to wonder if perhaps there would be no "settling of accounts." Or to even start thinking that the resources with which they'd been entrusted were really theirs by default. We do know that he eventually returned and made a careful examination of how much increase had been accomplished in his absence. You and I are in a similar situation. No one knows how long we have in this life. Nor do we know when Jesus is coming back to gather His followers to Himself. But the Bible makes it clear that when our time on earth is over, we'll owe our King an accounting of how much increase we've brought to His domain and how we've cared for the things placed under our control. Paul reminded the believers in Rome of the future day of accounting:

> Remember, we will all stand before the judgment seat of God. For the Scriptures say,
>
> "'As surely as I live,' says the LORD,
> 'every knee will bend to me,
> and every tongue will declare allegiance to God.'"

Yes, each of us will give a personal account to God. (Romans 14:10–12 NLT)

The day of our face-to-face meeting with our Master could come at any time. His arrival is neither scheduled nor predictable. All I know is that when that day comes, I want to hear the same words that greeted the ears of that five-talent steward:

Well done, good and faithful servant; you have been faithful over a few things, I will make you ruler over many things. Enter into the joy of your lord. (Matthew 25:23)

What a wonderful thing to have pronounced over your life by a King as gracious, good, and wonderful as our Lord Jesus. On the other hand, I certainly don't ever want to hear anything like what the master in the parable told the one-talent servant. I know you don't, either. It's so sobering I'm reluctant to even repeat the words. Yet Jesus spoke them, and the Holy Spirit saw to it they were faithfully recorded in the Word of God. There it is in our Bibles in red letters:

Therefore take the talent from him, and give it to him who has ten talents.

For to everyone who has, more will be given, and he will have abundance; but from him who does not have, even what he has will be taken away. And cast the unprofitable servant into the outer darkness. There will be weeping and gnashing of teeth. (Matthew 25:28–30)

As I said, the personal implications of bad stewardship are sobering—both for this life and for eternity. Poor stewards in this life don't get entrusted with more of God's resources. Nor do they experience the peace that comes from living without unnecessary stress and pressure, not to mention the sheer joy that results from getting to bless others freely and generously. That really is the most fun and most gratifying lifestyle available on planet earth today. Even better, living that way now sets us up for rewards in heaven. You see, being a poor steward won't keep you out of heaven. But the Bible makes it clear there are varying rewards available there. That's why Jesus encouraged us to "lay up for yourselves treasures in heaven, where neither moth nor rust destroys and where thieves do not break in and steal" (Matt. 6:20).

I'm sure you've heard of an investment vehicle called an IRA. The acronym stands for individual retirement account. Perhaps you have one. If so, good for you! It is a wise financial move to consistently make deposits into your IRA or Roth IRA. But what is the status of your ERA? Did you even know that you have an ERA? It stands for eternal retirement account, and it's the heavenly storehouse where you lay up treasure when you put God and the advancement of His kingdom first.

You can only make deposits into your ERA while you're on this earth. Some believers would be in trouble if they died today, because the deposits they've made are very meager. People who start making contributions to an IRA late in life have to double up to catch up. In a similar way, some people need to double up on their deposits to their ERA.

Here is wonderful news. No matter what kind of steward you've been up to this point in life—a one-talent, two-talent, or five-talent steward—you're not stuck in that category. You can move up! Start being faithful with what you currently have and you can be sure more will be entrusted to you!

Of course, if we want to avoid the fate of the one-talent steward, we need to ask ourselves a question: Why did the one-talent steward fail the test of stewardship? What was it about his mind-set or attitude that caused him to simply bury the talent entrusted to him, rather than, at minimum, putting it in the bank to draw interest?

The answer is right there in Jesus' remarkably detailed account of the conversation between the master and poor steward in His parable. Listen to the explanation the man puts forth on the day of accounting:

> Then he who had received the one talent came and said, "Lord, I knew you to be a hard man, reaping where you have not sown, and gathering where you have not scattered seed. And I was afraid, and went and hid your talent in the ground. Look, there you have what is yours." (Matthew 25:24–25)

"I was afraid," he said. A fear-driven approach to God—as opposed to a faith-driven, love-driven approach—is never a good starting place. "I knew you to be a hard man," he said. Yet God is good and kind and merciful and generous. In fact, the very opportunity to be His steward and experience the rewards of it is a product of His kindness and generosity. The one-talent steward told his master that he reaps where he hasn't sown, essentially accusing the master of unjustly profiting from the labor of others. Yet how can someone who owns everything reap where he hasn't sown?

He essentially makes an accusation of selfishness against the very person who is generously giving people who own nothing an opportunity to participate in his abundance. Not good. No wonder his excuse-making prompted such a harsh response from the returning ruler!

A wrong view of God will invariably lead you to a wrong

approach to stewardship of the things He has entrusted to you. For so many of God's people, the root of their inability to handle money and material possessions like stewards rather than owners is a simple lack of trust in God. They don't truly believe in their deepest souls that He is good and has their best interests at heart. They really believe they'll do a better job of looking out for their interests than the all-powerful, all-knowing Creator who loved them so much that He sent His only Son to die in their place.

In other words, they are like the one-talent servant, operating under the assumption that their master is hard, unfair, unjust, and uncaring.

How about you? Search your heart for the truth about how you view God. For many people, having grown up with a flawed, broken earthly father who was harsh, demanding, or simply

> Search your heart for the truth about how you view God.

unavailable makes it difficult to understand just how truly wonderful their heavenly Father is.

All you need to do is look to another parable of Jesus to get a glimpse of who your Father really is. Read Jesus' story of the prodigal son. It should really be called the parable of the wonderful father. There we see a father who gives his children the freedom to choose to be with him or walk away. A father always eagerly watching and waiting for his wayward child to return. And when his child does, he runs to meet him, throws his arms around him, and restores him to intimate fellowship.

God's not hard. He sowed something precious in you and He doesn't demand some set or exorbitant rate of return. He just asks you to recognize that you're His, and to be faithful. That means *to exercise faith*.

Trust Him with your finances and with your life. For He is trustworthy.

CHAPTER THREE

YOUR PERSPECTIVE OF PROVISION

In English, it officially goes by the name Old Yungas Road. Many consider it the most treacherous stretch of highway on planet earth.

Well, using the term *highway* is being generous. The forty-mile route linking Bolivia's capital La Paz to the city of Coroico in the Andes is basically a gravel road no wider than a single car in many spots. The route, frequently wet and muddy from tropical rains, hugs the mountainsides with sheer cliffs on the other side dropping many hundreds, sometimes thousands, of feet straight down. Did I mention there are no guardrails? The crumbling trail has earned a nickname from the local people. Estrada da Morte—that is, Road of Death. And with good reason. On average, more than two hundred people fall to their death in trucks, cars, and public buses each year on this road.

The most terrifying section of it—and based on the video I've seen, that's saying something—features sheer drop-offs on *both* sides of the narrow road, rather than just one. In this unbelievably dangerous stretch, the slightest driving mistake to either side—left or right—carries fatal consequences. Which brings me to why I'm mentioning Old Yungas Road in a book about managing resources.

You see, when it comes to money and wealth, the healthy, biblical road that leads to a life of blessing and impact has a treacherous ditch on each side. The bitter enemy of God that wants to keep you from having a big impact for His kingdom will do everything he can to get you to steer your thinking and attitudes about money into one of these two ditches. He doesn't really care which one you choose, because either will keep you from viewing and handling wealth in a healthy way. Please notice that I said "ditches," not cliffs. Failing to stay on this road isn't fatal. Unlike a wrong turn in the Bolivian Andes, this isn't a one-way trip. You can recover and get back on the road of healthy stewardship.

> Failing to stay on the road isn't fatal. You can receover and get back on the road of healthy stewardship.

These two ditches go by the names of Poverty Mind-Set and Prosperity Materialism Mind-Set. Behind both mistakes is a common spirit—an ancient, insidious demonic spirit to be precise. We'll name and shame that spirit later in this chapter. But for now, let's explore these two hazards so you can identify whether or not you're stuck in one.

The Poverty Mind-Set

The proverbial "vow of poverty." It has a very long history among Christians. The fact is that Christians have been promising God to remain poor for almost as long as there have been churches. And for understandable reasons. After all, didn't Jesus Himself tell the rich young ruler to sell everything if he wanted to inherit eternal life (Mark 10:17–22)? Didn't Jesus say it was easier for a camel to pass through the eye of a needle than for a rich man to get to heaven (Mark 10:25)?

He did indeed.

And didn't He also say, "Blessed are the poor"? And "Money is the root of all evil"?

Well, no, not really. But we'll get to those common misquotations in a moment. The fact remains that many believers are convinced that it is inappropriate—in fact, downright ungodly—for a Christian to have much in the way of success or material possessions in this world. Indeed, many are convinced they are earning points with God by living in poverty. But are these assumptions true? Biblical?

Let's call it the poverty mind-set—although in the Church history textbooks it goes under the fancier name *asceticism*.

In a very real sense, the Church was born on the day of Pentecost around AD 30. About 150 years later, the early Church father Tertullian was writing favorable things about Egyptian Christians who had renounced their claim to all earthly possessions and headed into the Egyptian desert to live in caves. Church historians agree that the monastic tradition among Christians was born there in Egypt around that time. Today the Egyptian deserts are sprinkled with the ancient remnants of the monasteries and enclaves of those cave-dwelling Christians. There are still a few active monasteries out there to this day.

About a thousand years later, Francis of Assisi took the theology of asceticism to the next level. Francis taught that it was actually a "virtue" to be poor. In a medieval Franciscan work titled "The Sacred

Exchange Between Saint Francis and Lady Poverty," the writer imagines Francis declaring that he wants to marry "Lady Poverty." In it we find:

> Holy poverty...is the foundation and guardian of all virtues...
> We have heard that you [Poverty] are the queen of virtues and,
> to some extent, we have learned this from experience.[1]

Francis ultimately founded the monastic order that bears his name, and to this day, joining the Franciscans requires taking a vow of poverty. This mind-set is rooted in the assumption that material possessions are inherently evil, or at least their ability to captivate us is so seductive and powerful that it is impossible to own anything without being corrupted by it. This belief isn't too far removed from the ancient heresy called *gnosticism*, which was a "dualistic" philosophy, meaning that it held that all matter was evil and that only spirit was good. Of course, this led the gnostics to reject the claim that Jesus was simultaneously both God and man. In their view, He couldn't be because matter is evil. Now, I'm not suggesting that Francis and his followers are gnostics. But I am suggesting that if you fall prey to the poverty mind-set, it's not a long leap to gnosticism from where you're standing.

Martin Luther, the medieval priest who became the father of the Protestant Reformation, was ultimately delivered from a poverty mind-set. After first entering the priesthood, Luther dove headfirst into asceticism, subjecting himself to severe discipline, even whipping himself to abstain from things he'd been taught were evil. He soon realized this was ineffective, moved from the monastery, and began to grow in his knowledge of God and His Word. Eventually, Luther would write, "If silver and gold are things evil in themselves, then those who keep away from them deserve to be praised. But if they are good creatures of God, which we can use both for the needs of our neighbor and for the glory of God, is not a person silly, yes, even unthankful to God, if he refrains from them as if they were evil?"[2]

Another aspect of this mind-set is the elevation of the world's poor to a sort of saintly status. This isn't mere concern and compassion for the poor, which every believer should exhibit. This is an extension of Francis of Assisi's religious exaltation of poverty as a holy virtue.

It's one thing to believe a poor person *can be* virtuous. (This is obviously true.) But it's another thing to consider someone virtuous *because* they're poor. Put another way, it's one thing to believe that poor people possess human dignity and value. (They do!) It's a big reach further to believe that there is a higher level of human dignity and value that only the poor possess. Yet this is essentially what religious asceticism teaches.

Today many Christians have absorbed some, if not all, of the ascetics' assumption that there is "virtue" in being poor—in other words, that you get points with God by not having anything. The implied flip side of this belief is that you *lose* points with God if you accumulate any wealth. This is the "ditch" of the poverty mind-set.

Is it any wonder that many of God's people are conflicted about money, success, achievement, and promotion? But is this really what the Bible teaches? Did Jesus' instructions to the rich young ruler indicate His expectation for every follower? And if so, why doesn't the Bible record Him giving the same directive to wealthy followers such as Nicodemus and Joseph of Arimathea?

By the way, Jesus did not say, "Blessed are the poor." In the Sermon on the Mount, He said, "Blessed are the poor in spirit, for theirs is the kingdom of heaven" (Matt. 5:3 NIV). In other words, those who recognize their spiritual bankruptcy and need of God will become blessed (happy) because God will enrich them with Himself! Money has nothing to do with any of that.

It's certainly true that we are not to love this world or the things of this world. The Bible is very clear about that. We are not to find our sense of significance or identity in possessions.' Instead, the believer's identity is rooted in being a child of God, and

> The believer's identity is rooted in being a child of God, and we're significant because God loved us and sent Jesus to redeem and restore us.

we're significant because God loved us and sent Jesus to redeem and restore us. Nor are we to root our hope or security in a bank balance or stock portfolio. Our security stems from the goodness and faithfulness of God and nothing else. This is precisely why Paul exhorted Timothy to encourage wealthy believers to keep their wealth in perspective:

> Command those who are rich in this present age not to be haughty, nor to trust in uncertain riches but in the living God, who gives us richly all things to enjoy. (I Timothy 6:17)

Notice the last part of Paul's instruction. We are to put our trust in the God who does what? "Gives us richly all things to enjoy." God wants us to enjoy His creation as long as we remember the first and most fundamental principle of stewardship—namely, that it is *His* creation. We enjoy things without "loving" them or elevating them to a higher place than they belong. Think about it. If you give a gift to your child, you don't want the child to start loving that gift more than you. You don't want the child to put her gift ahead of her relationship with you, or the future you're trying to give her. But you certainly want that child to enjoy it. You would be disappointed if she didn't! And in most cases, that's how children interact with their presents: They laugh and enjoy them, but not to the point of putting them ahead of their love for you.

That's how God wants us to approach His material gifts to us. They are truly gifts, and He wants us to enjoy them to their fullest. But He doesn't want us to derive our identity or sense of significance from them. This is likely what Jesus identified in the rich young ruler. He perceived, by the Spirit, that the young man's sense of identity was too deeply tied to his status and importance as a wealthy person. Jesus asked him to rid himself of that false identity, so He could show him who God really designed him to be. God doesn't mind us having things, but He never wants things to have us.

Asceticism takes this balanced "happy medium" to an unhappy extreme. This goes much further than recognizing the benefits of "fasting" certain luxuries from time to time, or feeling led to let go of something because it has begun to hold too high a place in the heart. This goes much further than giving something precious away in trust and faith because the Spirit of God prompted it. No, this is a warped view of life in God that drives the holder to a level of self-denial that deprives him or her of all but the basic necessities of life. Often at the root of this impulse is actually a form of religious pride. And at the root of *that* root, you'll find a spirit... the spirit of poverty.

The Symptoms of the Poverty Mind-Set

How can you know if you're in, or at least headed for, the ditch of a poverty mind-set? The answer is this: You will be hearing the spirit of poverty whispering certain messages to your mind. If you're in that ditch, you will have embraced and internalized several of these interrelated messages:

The spirit of poverty tells us that stuff comes from the devil.

This is simply the modern, updated version of the gnostic heresy. It's a lie, yet many believers operate as if money and material things are inherently evil and corrupting. The fact is they are neutral. They take on the characteristics of whoever controls them. We have already seen that all of creation rightly belongs to God. In the hands of one of His children, operating as a faithful steward, wealth and resources become assets in His kingdom. If, however, stuff comes from the devil, then all increase, profit, or growth in this area must be from him. Which leads us to our next symptom:

The spirit of poverty tells us to be ashamed of our stuff.

We're basically logical creatures. So, if we start with an assumption that all wealth, increase, and material possessions are intrinsically evil and come from the devil or the devil's system, then it follows logically that any Christian with a conscience would feel a sense of shame about having any of these things. And indeed many do.

Many—in fact, I suspect *most*—believers aren't quite convinced enough by the spirit of poverty to give away everything and join a monastery, yet they are convinced enough that they feel ashamed of any of the good things that come their way. Which leads us to this next symptom:

The spirit of poverty tries to make us think that we paid less than we really did.

When a friend compliments you on a new item—it could be anything from a new shirt or blouse to a car—do you instantly feel the need to downplay the cost of the item? When you hear the words, "Ooh, nice watch!" do you blush and instantly feel the need to explain how you got a great deal on it or how it was a gift from someone else? If you tend to feel a reflexive spasm of shame when someone notices something nice that you possess, you have likely embraced some or all of the deception of the spirit of poverty. In a similar way...

> The spirit of poverty makes us feel the need to justify all our purchases.

"I need a nicer car because I frequently need to transport clients; otherwise, I'd be perfectly happy with an old heap."

"The strap broke on my old purse, so I finally had to break down and get another one."

"We didn't really want to buy a bigger house, but we felt like we had to have more space for Bible studies and small groups."

If these sound familiar at all, then you're probably also familiar with this related symptom:

> The spirit of poverty tries to make us feel guilty for God's blessings.

"Hey, I heard about your promotion. Congratulations!"

"Aw, well... you know... it was just... thanks."

The fact is that our God is a God of growth and increase. As we've already seen, His initial marching orders to Adam and Eve were to "be fruitful and multiply" (Gen. 1:28) and cultivate the garden, which would cause it to bear more fruit. And as we saw in the parable of the stewards, He expects His stewards to multiply what He has entrusted to them. Furthermore, doing things God's way—applying biblical principles and divine wisdom to every aspect of life and work—invariably results in increase and growth. Things simply go better when we do them God's way. Yet the spirit of poverty would have us view this increase with suspicion or even guilt.

Simplification Is Not Asceticism

Before I go too much further, let me state emphatically that for many believers—especially in places like the United States—a significant "house cleansing" and shedding of "stuff" can be an important step in getting out of the other ditch, the prosperity materialism mind-set, which we will explore shortly. The ditch of a poverty mind-set is something far different from the very healthy desire to simplify your life, shed unhealthy material attachments, or temporarily "fast" some luxury in order to focus on God.

Frankly, many of us are drowning in stuff and could benefit greatly from more simplicity in our lives, and in our homes. Knowing how to simplify and make do with less is also vital when you're getting out of debt or beginning to live within your means.

As we'll soon see in our examination of materialism, it's vital that we reject our culture's idolatrous obsession with accumulating things. Contrary to what the bumper sticker suggests, it's not "he who dies with the most toys" who wins. The eternal winners are those who enter heaven having been faithful stewards of what God entrusted to their care.

God designed us to inhabit a wondrously made physical body that lives in an amazingly beautiful world. And

> It's vital that we reject our culture's idolatrous obsession with accumulating things.

He invites us to enjoy it all in a spirit of gratitude and joy. Although we're not created to worship or invest ultimate love in the things we touch, taste, see, hear, and smell, we are meant to fully enjoy them as generous gifts from our Father.

The Prosperity Materialism Mind-Set

As you already know, the road of rightly relating to money and things has a ditch on the other side, as well. It's not just the error of the poverty mind-set that you need to avoid. We have seen that the other hazard is giving money and material things a place in your heart that only God is supposed to occupy. Materialism takes a good thing that God gives us and makes it an ultimate thing. In the same way that many Christians have embraced a poverty mind-set, many Christians have embraced a materialistic mind-set known as the prosperity gospel.

This second pitfall is a philosophy that says, "I need to accumulate as much money and things as I possibly can no matter the cost." It's embedded and reflected in our popular culture in the form of sayings like, *You only live once* and *Get all you can and can all you get.* And, as I've already mentioned, *The one who dies with the most toys wins!*

Allow me to share a few quotes from some historical figures:

1. "I have made many millions but they have not brought me happiness."
2. "The care of 200 million is enough to kill anyone. There's no pleasure in it."
3. "I am the most miserable man on earth."

4. "I was happier when I was doing a mechanic's job."
5. "Millionaires seldom smile."

Now let's match the quote with the man who uttered it:

1. John D. Rockefeller: founder of Standard Oil; richest person in history.
2. W. H. Vanderbilt: railroad tycoon; world's richest man in 1877.
3. John Jacob Astor: America's first multimillionaire.
4. Henry Ford: founder, Ford Motor Company.
5. Andrew Carnegie: industrialist; second-richest man in history.

It's stunning to contemplate that the wealthiest men of the nineteenth and twentieth centuries testified that wealth can't deliver any of the things that give life meaning and joy. Yet millions continue to be seduced by the glittering allure of materialism.

In many ways it is the mirror image of the poverty mind-set. Whereas the spirit of poverty tells you that stuff comes from the devil, materialism convinces you that you earned it and deserve it. Whereas the spirit of poverty tells you to be ashamed of your stuff, materialism says to be proud of it and flaunt it. And whereas the spirit of poverty tries to make people think that you paid less than you really did, materialism wants others to think you spent more.

This mind-set is very much tied to what Jesus, in his parable of the soils, called "the deceitfulness of riches" (Mark 4:19). Something that is "deceitful" tells lies. What do riches lie about? The spirit of materialism constantly whispers falsehoods such as these:

"Significance and security come from having money and nice things."

"If you had a little more money, you'd finally be happy."

"You're falling behind. Others are doing better than you."

"More money would solve your problems."

"Your hard work, cleverness, and initiative are solely responsible for your success."

None of these statements are true, yet they are unquestioningly integrated into the thinking and belief system of countless Christians. But why? What feeds these falsehoods? I have a few thoughts about this.

The Fuel of Materialism

Not long ago I read the results of a research study that estimated that by the age of twenty, the average American young person has already been exposed to more than one million commercial messages. The vast majority of these messages were expertly crafted to deliver one or more of the spirit of materialism's numerous, seductive lies. Those lies include the following:

You need more.

You deserve more.

You're incomplete unless you get more.

You'd be happier if you had more.

The Bible has three special terms to describe the dark feelings and impulses that these messages stir up. John sternly warned believers about them when he wrote, "For all that is in the world—the lust of the flesh, the lust of the eyes, and the pride of life—is not of the Father but is of the world" (I John 2:16).

Did you catch it? The three were (1) the lust of the flesh, (2) the lust of the eyes, and (3) the boastful pride of life. Advertising agencies earn their billions each year instilling these three dark cravings into the souls of unsuspecting viewers and listeners. And the age of social media has only added another powerful weapon to the spirit of materialism's arsenal. Spend a little time on any of the popular social media platforms and you'll soon be convinced that everyone in the world has a better life than you; is living in a better house than you, with rooms that look as if they were lifted from the pages of a magazine; is eating at better restaurants than you; and is taking better vacations than you. The reality is you're only seeing the very best of the best on social media. The lives of others are much less ideal in reality.

Materialism takes a good thing that God gives us and makes it an ultimate thing. It attaches our *self-worth* to our *net worth*. It actually stunts and even destroys our spiritual lives. It wrenches our focus away from God and places it on objects. It blinds us to the curses of wealth. And it invariably ends in futility. It will never lead to true joy and fulfill-

> True blessings can only come from relationship with God and becoming the person He created you to be for *His* purposes.

ment. Those blessings can only come from relationship with God and becoming the person He created you to be for *His* purposes.

The spirit of materialism leaves us miserable, alienated from others, and separated from God—alone in every way.

The Common Link

Two ditches. Two mirror-image forms of deception. The enemy of your soul doesn't really care which one you choose, as long as he can get you off the road of faithful stewardship. They both ensnare you into a destructive focus on *things*. Granted, they do this through opposite propositions, but the net effect is the same. Instead of pursuing your surrender to, and relationship with, Christ, these two traps take your eyes off Him and place them on *stuff*. One does it through valuing it too little, the other through valuing it too highly.

With either one, you've given money a place in your life it should not have. With either one, you'll be robbed of all the peace, contentment, and fun God wants you to enjoy; and God's kingdom will be robbed of the impact you were meant to have in the world.

These two twisted mind-sets have more in common than you might imagine. At the root of both is a single, evil spiritual force. Yes, that's right; I'm talking about a demonic spirit. Jesus Himself identified this spirit by name. He called it "Mammon."

In one of Jesus' landmark statements on money in Matthew 6:24, He says, "No one can serve two masters; for either he will hate the one and love the other, or else he will be loyal to the one and despise the other. You cannot serve God and mammon" (KJV).

It is noteworthy that Jesus uses the Greek word *mammonas* here, which is a transliteration of the Aramaic word meaning "treasure" or "riches." This is a completely different word for riches than He used in Mark 4:19 where He warned about "the deceitfulness of riches." There, the word for riches is *ploutos*. The reason becomes clear when you understand that Mammon was also the name of a Chaldean "god of riches." It is clear from Jesus' statement that Mammon wants to be served like a false god. (Going all the way back to the Garden of Eden, the devil and his cohort have always been about trying to draw our worship away from the one place it truly belongs.) Mammon is an actual spirit that has been exploiting human greed, envy, and fear of lack since the dawn of history.

Keep in mind the name Babylon is derived from Babel—as in, the ancient tower humans built to try to raise themselves to God's level. The spirit behind Babel is actually the same as the core impulse behind Mammon. The builders of Babel told themselves, "We don't need God. We can be like Him. Self-sufficient. Independent." As you may recall, this impulse was at the heart of the original deception that caused the fall of humankind and creation in the first place (see Gen. 3:5).

Now, I know many of us put the word *money* in there for *mammon* when citing that verse, but truthfully, if Jesus wanted to say *money*, He would have said it. He used the word *mammon* because even the Jewish people had succumbed to serving this false god. Jesus knew the invisible spiritual dynamic working behind the scenes.

Mammon is looking for servants by trying to take the place of God. It promises us everything that only God can give us. Mammon says, *If you had more money, people would listen to you. If you had more money, you would have significance in the world. If you had more money, you could live a better life and you'd be happier. If you had more money, you would have security.*

Yes, Mammon promises things only God can provide. In other words, Mammon wants to take the place of God.

So, in a very real sense, Mammon is actually an anti-Christ spirit. Why make such a bold statement? Because when the book of Revelation talks about "the beast" (the anti-Christ), it warns that his source of power and control is economic rather than military. He does not rule through the threat of nuclear war, but through the threat of not being able to buy or sell (see Rev. 13). In other words, he rules through the threat of the control of money. That threat only has power over people who love and crave money more than they love and revere God.

> When we define God's love for us in financial terms, suspect that God loves us more when we have more money, and wonder if He loves us less when our bank account is low, we're serving Mammon instead of Him.

The spirit of Mammon fights to usurp God's place in our lives by promising things that only God can truly provide: things like security, provision, and ultimate purpose in life. That's why greed is one of Mammon's most common, and most destructive, manifestations. When we define God's love for us in financial terms, suspect that God loves us more when we have more money, and wonder if He loves us less when our bank account is low, we're serving Mammon instead of Him. Remember that Jesus made it perfectly clear: We cannot serve both. We have to choose.

Our enemy is constantly trying to confuse us on this point. He's always whispering in our ears to move us into either a poverty or materialism mind-set. It might be a message like:

Go ahead and put the pursuit of wealth first in your life right now. Once you get rich through your own efforts, then you'll be free to put God's agenda first. Your wealth will be a sign that God is pleased with you.

Or it could be one like:

God doesn't want His people to have anything in this life. All your rewards are in heaven. See all those wealthy Christians over there? They're sellouts. They're compromisers. You're a better Christian than they are.

The fact is for every way we can serve God, there is a counterfeit way to serve Mammon. Both the prosperity gospel and the poverty gospel are counterfeits—and both serve Mammon by taking our eyes off God and investing our trust and our focus on ourselves and material things.

If you teach your children that money is the answer to their problems, they will grow up to serve money—literally, to serve Mammon. And according to Jesus Himself, as a result they won't serve God. Why? Because He flatly declared you can't serve both.

Again, Mammon runs seamlessly between materialism and asceticism! The spirit of greed/materialism tells us that stuff means everything. It tells us to be proud of our stuff. The spirit of poverty tries to make us feel guilty for God's blessings! It tells us that stuff comes from the devil, and that we should be ashamed of anything we have.

Either way, it keeps your eye, your attention, and your heart firmly rooted in how you deal with *stuff.*

The Middle of the Road: Living "on Mission"

So, what is the answer? How does God want us to think about and relate to wealth and material possessions? Put another way, how do we stay on Stewardship Road?

It starts with the fundamental assumption that we established in chapter 1—namely, that God owns it all. All of creation belongs to Him.

Here is stewardship boiled down to its purest essence:

- I put God first in everything because He loves me and redeemed me.
- I gratefully receive everything God puts in my hand.

- I steward faithfully what He has entrusted to me.
- I hold His blessings with an open hand, prepared to give or distribute them as He directs, never forgetting that they are His, and that I am His.

That's it! That's Stewardship Road. That's living free of Mammon's ugly influence.

God wants to bless you. It's His nature as a good Father. But His blessings extend much further than your pocketbook. He absolutely desires you to thrive and do well in every area of life—spirit, soul, and body. Now, the common term for doing well in every area of life is *prosperity*, but that has become a loaded, misunderstood term in Christian circles, so I try to avoid it.

In God's economy, from the vantage point of eternity, blessing isn't measured in material things. His blessing isn't counted in dollars. Godly prosperity actually means having the wind of God's Spirit in your sails as you move through life. It's having Him get behind you—to propel you. It means to grow or increase. To move forward.

Above all, the faithful steward never forgets that the ultimate wealth, and the ultimate blessing, is Him. God's presence, favor, and love are actually more precious than any material substance. I know you hear this a lot in Christian circles—so often that it can sound like a cliché. Nevertheless, the greatest reward, by far, of being a believer is relationship with God.

Truly, some things are so precious that their value is not only impossible to measure but outwardly invisible and apparently nonexistent. God's love, for example, doesn't feel valuable in a world that only measures what we can see and visibly measure. From the standpoint of eternity, however—the unseen realm where flesh doesn't exist and the spirit is no longer invisible—His presence is valuable beyond calculation. Here, none of the things the people in this fallen world hold precious mean a thing. In heaven, gold is just a street-paving material.

In Mark 10:21, Jesus told the rich young ruler, "One thing you lack: Go your way, sell whatever you have and give to the poor, and you will have treasure in heaven; and come, take up the cross, and follow Me. The young man was sad at this word and went away sorrowful, for he had great possessions." He was sad because, in Jesus' eyes, he didn't have stuff—his stuff *had him*.

It is not God's will for us to be poor—nor is it necessarily God's will that all His people be rich (whatever that means—I've been to villages in other parts of the world where being "rich" meant having a cow *and* a goat). It is God's will for us to be blessed so we can be a blessing. He wants us to have all our needs supplied with plenty leftover to help others. It is God's will to see more people come into relationship with Him.

You see, contrary to what many would have us believe, the gospel is not a poverty gospel. Nor is it, as some preachers and teachers would have us think, a prosperity gospel. No, the good news of life in Jesus Christ is a provision gospel. This frees us to live a lifestyle of generosity wherein we experience "all sufficiency in all things" so that we "have an abundance for every good work" (2 Cor. 9:8).

I believe the Bible calls us to live our life *on mission*. Living on mission means that we don't focus on ourselves and our desires but on what God is doing in the world and how we can partner with His work. It does not mean life without joy, or an enjoyment of the material blessings He gives us. It does mean living with an awareness that heaven is our home—and that we're just pilgrims passing through this world.

> Good stewards are free to be outwardly focused because they're confident in God's provision and protection.

Put as simply as I know how… stuff is stuff. God is not into stuff. God is into hearts. The key to stewardship is not putting your focus on getting more. Nor is it a focus on having less. The goal is to focus on God with gratitude and joy in the privilege of knowing Him. At the same time, how we think about money and material things does expose the true condition of our hearts.

Good stewards are free to be outwardly focused because they're confident in God's provision and protection. We can be focused on God's agenda because we're so confident in His love, care, and faithfulness. David Livingstone, the famous pioneering missionary to Africa, understood this. He once wrote,

I place no value on anything I have or may possess, except in relation to the kingdom of God. If anything will advance the interests of the kingdom, it shall be given away or kept, only as by giving or keeping it I shall most promote the glory of Him to whom I owe all my hopes in time or eternity.[3]

That's the path of stewardship.

CHAPTER FOUR

THE CFO OF "YOU, INC."

Let's start with a parable. But first let me give away the ending. (Spoiler alert!) This is an illustration of how and why you're the chief financial officer of a wholly owned subsidiary of the universe's biggest enterprise. You're the star of this movie, so let's start with a little backstory.

Imagine you grew up as a runaway—alone, wandering, alienated and angry, totally impoverished. As a teenager, you seethed with so much resentment and rebellion that you often broke onto the nearby grounds of your king's estate and vandalized its beautiful, manicured gardens and facilities. You slept in its barn. You stole food from its storehouse. You escalated to throwing rocks through its windows and spray-painting graffiti onto its walls.

Eventually, you were caught and arrested. With all the king's power, and so much damage inflicted, he could have easily had you executed. But to your astonishment, instead of pressing charges...

He paid for your defense. He paid your fines.

He forgave you.

Not only did he save your life, but he bought your freedom and gave it back to you—no strings attached.

Then he elevated his compassion and generosity to an even higher level. He actually adopted you into his family! The king became your father.

Your new dad didn't treat you as a second-class offspring, either. He gave you a place near the head of the table and treated you in every way like his other kids. He put his money where his mouth was by even changing his will to make you a full coheir with his other children of his vast fortune (more than you could ever spend).

When you grow up, he takes it a step further—a step that's the whole point of this story. He takes you into his family business.

This father knows that it's vital that his children learn how to administrate, manage, and govern, because his domain is ever growing and expanding. Plus, he just enjoys working with his kids! So, he doesn't just give you a menial job but actually entrusts you with management responsibility for one of his smaller subsidiary companies. But he doesn't just throw you into the deep end of the pool hoping you'll figure out how to swim. He gives you a book full of wisdom and insight on how an enterprise should be run. Plus, he's never more than a phone call away to answer a question or provide counsel. But he's primarily interested in seeing what you do with this opportunity, so he doesn't force you to follow his wisdom. He respects your decision-making power.

As you start to succeed—and he defines success by serving his customers well and expanding the mission of the enterprise—he's incredibly generous with his compensation package. It turns out he truly loves lavishing good things on his kids.

Sound familiar? It should. This is very much a parallel story to

Jesus' parable of the three stewards we examined in chapter 2. I also hope it raises several important questions in your mind. The truth is that you are the chief financial officer of "You, Inc.," a wholly owned subsidiary within God's universal holding company called The Kingdom.

> You are the chief financial officer of "You, Inc.," a wholly owned subsidiary within God's universal holding company called The Kingdom.

You wear a lot of titles in God's Kingdom. Son or daughter, child of God, heir, beloved, treasure, friend. Of course, the title of CFO is a completely modern one, but it's one of your titles nonetheless.

"Are you sure, Robert?" you may be thinking. "Show me that in the Word." Fair enough. The fact is we'll see this concept running as a thread from Genesis to Revelation. But there is one passage in particular I want to point you to before we dive into the details of this role.

In 1 Corinthians 9:17, the apostle Paul, as rendered in the old King James Version, says,

> For if I do this thing willingly, I have a reward: but if against my will, *a dispensation of the gospel* is committed unto me. (emphasis added)

Behind that old English word *dispensation* in that verse is the Greek word *oikonomia*, the root of our English words *economy* and *economics*. Strong's New Testament Greek lexicon defines *oikonomia* as "the management of a household or of household affairs; specifically, the management, oversight, administration, of other's property." It's the very word the ancient Greeks would have used to describe a person left in charge of the management and operation of a ranch, farm, shop, or business enterprise.

Isn't it interesting that Paul chose to use this particular word when describing what God had called him to do? He said he'd been given a "dispensation of the gospel." The New King James Version translates that same phrase as "I have been entrusted with a stewardship." And this isn't the only time Paul described his life's work as an *oikonomia*. In Ephesians 3:2, he said he had been given a "dispensation of the grace of God." And in Colossians 1:25 Paul writes,

Whereof I am made a minister, according to the dispensation of God which is given to me for you, to fulfill the word of God. (KJV)

Without a doubt, Paul viewed his life and calling in terms of stewarding a spiritual business enterprise that God had entrusted to him. In the light of this and Jesus' numerous stewardship parables, shouldn't we do so as well?

You might read this and think, *But I'm not good at business finance. This isn't my skill set.* Or even, *I'm bad at math!* Relax. Finance doesn't have to be your strong suit—because this is far from your ordinary CFO position. The principles of stewardship are simple and straightforward. Besides, as I've already noted, once you step out in faith to do things in alignment with God's ways and wisdom, you'll find a supernatural heavenly wind at your back. Jesus didn't call the Holy Spirit "the Helper" for nothing.

Furthermore, you're not reporting to a typical chairman of the board.

Your Boss

One thing many people fail to grasp about God is that He loves to delegate authority and responsibility to His people. From the very beginning, God invited His first created son and daughter into His highest work. Remember that humanity's original job was to tend the garden and expand it across the whole of planet earth. What was true back in the garden remained true when Jesus announced the launch of God's program of restoring what the Fall had broken. Just as God had told Adam and Eve to be fruitful, multiply, and extend their dominion everywhere, Jesus, following His resurrection, essentially told His disciples the same thing:

> From the very beginning, God invited His first created son and daughter into His highest work.

All authority has been given to Me in heaven and on earth. Go therefore and make disciples of all the nations, baptizing them in the name of the Father and of the Son and of the Holy Spirit, teaching them to observe all things that I have commanded you; and lo, I am with you always, even to the end of the age. (Matthew 28:18–20)

Notice how in the Great Commission Jesus delegates His authority to His followers. He could have won the world on His own, but He chooses to invite us to join Him. He accomplishes His goals through us so we can experience the joy, meaning, and rewards with Him.

What this all says about God is truly stunning. Our heavenly Father doesn't do this out of insecurity, a lack of knowledge, or an inability to do it all Himself. He does this as a good teacher and boss who practices hands-on learning. He also does this as a loving Father who considers His children's learning and growth as equally important to the official "job at hand."

Best of all, I think He does this as not just a "Father" but a "Daddy" who actually delights in the company of His kids—especially when the kids have chosen to come home and be with Him and to make what's important to Him, important to them.

I have a news flash—your heavenly Daddy not only loves you but delights in your company! He savors watching you walk and grow and stretch your emerging abilities just as deeply as we love watching our toddlers stumble through their first steps. God relishes trusting you with other treasures He's created, and watching you bask in the blessings they bring to your life. It brings a smile to His face to watch you co-labor with Him in the great work of redemption He's carrying out in the world.

Even though He owns everything you are and everything you touch, He's put it all in your hands for safekeeping and growth. He's even given you an incredible working environment—His beautiful creation of the natural world.

There really is no getting around it. Your life is an enterprise, and you're an honest-to-goodness CFO. That means you're solely responsible for how the money is handled in your own personal *oikonomia*. Here is the potentially awkward or painful question that you must ask yourself: If you were to receive a performance evaluation right now, would you be anticipating a promotion? A demotion? A termination?

I ask, not to shame you or make you feel bad. But as anyone

who's successfully been through a twelve-step program for breaking an addiction will tell you, the process of real change can only begin with fearless, gut-level honest assessment of your current ways. The wonderful news is that, starting today, you can become an outstanding CFO. The kind of manager whose wise stewardship continually qualifies you for ever-increasing levels of responsibility and impact in the larger enterprise. And here's more good news.

Your boss is incredibly patient, kind, and gracious. He makes it easy to succeed. You fail in this job primarily by refusing to begin or acknowledge it. As with almost everything in God, it's all about your heart.

Of course, like any good boss, He tends to start you off slowly. You wouldn't want to be thrown into the job of running a multinational corporation on your first day, would you? You may be headed straight for the top, you may be bursting with aptitude and diligence, but even winners have to work their way up. In this case, think of God having given you primary control of a small branch. Recall that in any small enterprise, the manager wears a lot of hats. Sometimes he or she serves the customers, cleans up the store, takes deliveries, and even makes the product. That's the challenge of early days.

Good Bosses Do Performance Evaluations

Remember Luke 16:10: "He who is faithful in what is least is faithful also in much; and he who is unjust in what is least is unjust also in much." Big or small amounts can test your heart with equal rigor—because again, it's about your heart, not the amounts. It's about whether you're being "faithful"—literally whether you're acting out of faith and trust in Him, or out of something else: fear, greed, or even resentment. Remember the unfaithful steward in the parable of the talents, who reacted out of fear that was itself born out of distrust and resentment of the owner? He accused the owner of being a hard and unjust man. And I cannot state this emphatically enough...

God is neither hard nor unjust. Ever.

> God is neither hard nor unjust. Ever.

His anger against sin can be fierce, precisely because He knows the awful toll sin takes on the people He loves. But He is never unkind. He *is* love. And He is the very embodiment of justice—the benchmark against which justice defines its very existence. Injustice is the complete opposite of God's nature.

So, isn't it ironic that *unjust* and *unfair* are what His enemy accuses your heavenly Father of being? It's what the devil insinuated to Eve that caused the catastrophic fall of humankind. *God is holding out on you. He's holding you back.* And that's also exactly what he whispers into your ear, urging you to believe. God's bitter enemy, and yours, is the father of lies. And perhaps the big lie for all the ages is the smear that God is unjust. Unfair. Unkind.

The truth is that God is infinitely just, fair, and kind. Yet as we've already seen, a day of accounting comes for all of us. In other words, in your role as the CFO of You, Inc., a big, ultimate performance review lies ahead at the end of your life, but until then, the quality of your stewardship is being constantly monitored by a loving Father-God Chairman of the Board. The quality of that stewardship determines whether your portfolio gets expanded or reduced.

Please understand that when the resources entrusted to a poor steward are reduced, this is not God being mean or hard. This is

His kindness in operation. Increasing the resources available to a poor steward would damage both the steward and hamper the vital progress of God's kingdom activity on earth. That activity is redemptive. The eternal destinies of billions of souls hang in the balance. The kingdom of God on earth is an enterprise created to share the gospel with every person.

God's passionate love for people compels Him to redirect resources to the hands of those who will partner with Him in the most important cause on earth. This is a cause so dear to Him that He was willing to sacrifice His own, beloved Son in order to make it possible.

I don't know about you, but knowing that my stewardship is being examined from heaven makes me want to examine it myself. After all, good managers constantly evaluate the health of their own enterprises.

What about your time? Yes, good, faithful stewards are wise managers of the only truly scarce resource on planet earth: time. Wealth can be created. Indeed, wealth is created and expands all the time. Yet there are only 1,440 minutes in a day. You, me, Bill Gates, Warren Buffett…we all get the same number each day and not a single minute more.

> Good, faithful stewards are wise managers of the only truly scarce resource on planet earth: time.

No Rewards for Maintaining

Have the other assets God entrusted to you—your body, your soul, your life, your relationships, your family, your natural giftings, your possessions—been well managed? Are all those assets growing, or at least producing a growing impact on God's kingdom? You will recall that in the parable of the three stewards, the unfaithful steward returned all of the owner's money. But simply maintaining or hoarding his assets wasn't viewed as acceptable by the master. On the contrary, the returning owner castigated the one-talent steward in the harshest imaginable way. The whole thing is rather shocking to our modern, democratic, American way of thinking.

I recall reading this passage one time and thinking, "Wow, Lord. Couldn't the owner have at least commended the poor guy for not losing any money? After all, I know a lot of smart, professional investors and money managers who lost a lot of their clients' nest eggs in the dot-com crash of 2000 and the global financial crisis in 2008. Could he not at least have gotten some sort of consolation prize for not losing ground? Maybe just a 'participation trophy' or something?"

But that's not how the parable goes, is it? Two of the stewards brought increase to the master's assets. One merely maintained what he had been given. The lesson of Jesus' parable is that the Lord does not view maintaining as faithfulness. Maintaining is not rewarded. Only increase—taking new ground—is praised as "good and faithful."

After the accounting is done, the owner scolds the timid, fearful, lazy steward for not, at minimum, putting his money in a bank where it could draw interest. The harshness of the condemnation received by Mr. Maintainer is pretty stunning in itself. But I find what the master does next even more amazing. As we've seen, he then takes the one and only talent from the one-talent guy and hands it over to the guy who already has ten talents! At that point in Jesus' story, the owner explains his remarkable instruction: "For to everyone who has, more will be given, and he will have abundance; but from him who does not have, even what he has will be taken away" (Matt. 25:29). My natural mind just finds that so surprising.

Now, at first blush this can seem like it solidly confirms the cynical, resentful old adage about the rich getting richer and the poor getting poorer. That's certainly what it sounds like. Of course, that's the complete opposite of how the majority of us modern, equality-minded, sensitive folks would handle the situation. Think about it. Here's this clearly not-too-on-the-ball guy with one measly talent to manage, and the owner takes it away from him...and gives it to Mr. Ten Talents! He could have at least given it to Four-Talent Guy (who, I guess, represents the middle class in this economics lesson). But no, the owner seemingly takes from the poor, skips the middle class, and gives to the rich. He's the anti–Robin Hood!

I'm joking here, of course. That is not at all the message of this parable. The lesson here has absolutely nothing to do with rich and poor. You'll recall that each steward had initially been given resources in accordance with the stewardship ability they had demonstrated in the past. And in the parable, each one had a fresh, new chance to elevate the level of their stewardship. The simple but tough takeaway here is that good stewards are entrusted with more and bad stewards are entrusted with less.

By the way, the Bible is clear that God's heart is very much toward the poor. In fact, the Word of God makes it clear from cover to cover that if you want to get God's attention, show generosity and compassion for three special groups of people—the poor, orphans, and widows. Anyone

> Anyone who, from a pure heart, endeavors to extend compassion and care to "the least of these" will find God smiling on them.

who, from a pure heart, endeavors to extend compassion and care to "the least of these" will find God smiling on them. It's a good idea to remain mindful that God takes the plight of widows and orphans very seriously.

I vividly remember one instance in which the Spirit of God reminded Debbie and me of this principle. We were house hunting and found one we felt the Lord wanted us to buy. Now, anyone who knows me will tell you I'm a bargain hunter. Actually, I believe that a key part of my stewardship responsibility is to avoid overpaying for the things we purchase. So once we found a house we both were at peace about buying, I was about to instruct our real estate agent to make an aggressively low offer on it to get the negotiations started. When I checked with Debbie about it, she said, "Robert, you'd better check and make sure that it's not a widow who owns the house." What a wise wife God gave me! Knowing how God feels about the plight of widows and orphans, the last thing either of us wanted to be part of was taking advantage of a widow in a difficult situation.

So, I called our agent and said, "Okay, I have what may sound like an unusual question. I know you guys are taught to keep buyers and sellers as far apart as possible. But I need to know if the seller is a widow." I may have held my breath a little waiting for the answer. Why? Because Debbie and I both knew that if the answer was yes, we were going to make a full, asking-price offer. The agent said, "No, it's a middle-aged man." I think my response was, "Whew!" Then my agent asked why I wanted to know. I said, "Because if it was a widow, we were about to way overpay for that house. We don't mess with widows. God has their back!"

No, the lesson of Jesus' parable of the three stewards is not that God takes from the poor and gives to the rich. It *is* clearly declaring that God takes from bad stewards and gives to good stewards. I'm sorry if that seems hard to you, but think about it. Why would God direct influence, wealth, treasure, and opportunity to someone He knows is going to squander it? When he looks down from heaven, what is He looking for? He's looking for good stewards. He's looking for servants He can bless. Why?

Because God is a good steward, too! He wants to faithfully steward His Son's immense sacrifice! Jesus willingly shed His innocent blood to bring the lost back into relationship with a loving Father God. So, God seeks to maximize Jesus' enormous investment. He does so by directing more resources to His children who manage their finances in such a way that they have plenty leftover to give to their local church and to other organizations that are reaching the unreached. Also, as we've just seen, God's heart is for the poor, the orphan, and the widow. His heart is for people in desperate circumstances. So, he's looking for faithful, obedient individuals and families He can bless who will reflect His heart of compassion for those people.

In other words, God is not punishing bad stewards to be mean or harsh. God is looking for good stewards because He loves people!

For additional insight, let's revisit Luke 16:10–12. Jesus said,

> God is looking for good stewards because He loves people!

He who is faithful in what is least is faithful also in much; and he who is unjust in what is least is unjust also in much. Therefore, if you have not been faithful in the unrighteous mammon, who will commit to your trust the true riches? And if you have not been faithful in what is another man's, who will give you what is your own?

Now, let me give you the Robert Morris Condensed Paraphrase Version (RMCPV) of the first of these three verses: "If God can't trust you with a little, He can't trust you with a lot." That's essentially what Jesus is saying in verse 10.

We're very good at conning ourselves. Most poor stewards tell themselves that if they only had a little more money, *then* they would be prudent, generous, and put God first in their finances. "If I were better off, I'd be a better steward," they think. But that simply isn't true. Jesus knew and clearly stated that if you're not a good steward with a little, you won't be a good steward with a lot. And you'll never be entrusted with a lot until you learn to steward what you have. Never.

Here is the RMCPV of verse 11, which talks about "unrighteous mammon" and "true riches": "If I can't trust you with mere money (which will perish), I certainly can't trust you with ministry (which is much more important because it's eternal)." What are true riches? True riches are ministering to people, helping people, loving people. God says, "For heaven's sake, if I can't trust you with a dollar bill, I certainly can't trust you with a priceless soul!"

Until we learn to steward this very unrighteous part of our lives (money), we're not going to be trustworthy stewards of the most holy and sacred part of our mission and calling here on earth (kingdom things).

Finally, in verse 12 Jesus is basically saying, "If you're not faithful with what someone else entrusts to you, I'm sorry, but I can't give you your own." In other words, if you're not a good employee, you wouldn't be a good employer.

> If you're not a good employee, you wouldn't be a good employer.

Are you beginning to get the idea that being a good steward is an important thing in the eyes of God? Is it becoming clear that this is a vital set of skills, habits, and values to possess if you want to be and do everything God has called you to be and do? I hope so. In the next section of the book we'll get down to the nitty-gritty of how to do that. But for now let me tell you something I've learned about good stewards. I've known lots of outstanding, successful stewards in God's kingdom over the years. I've carefully observed their lives and disciplines because I wanted to learn from them. In the process I've discovered that all good stewards do three things:

- They spend wisely.
- They save diligently.
- They give generously.

It's really that simple. Of course, there is a lot of detail, strategy, and wisdom to unpack within each of those three items and we'll do just that on the pages ahead. But for now, let's close this chapter by reviewing, to make sure you understand a vital truth.

You Are the Only CFO You, Inc., Has

You are the chief financial officer of your one-and-only life. If you're married, you and your spouse hold that position jointly for your household. Your little enterprise is an important part of a much larger conglomerate. According to Colossians 1:13, when God saved you, he rescued you from the domain of darkness and transferred you into the kingdom of His beloved Son. The tricky thing about being a subsidiary in this kingdom is that it is largely invisible. It is spiritual. Heavenly. And an invisible God is enthroned at the head of a very long conference table.

Your Founder and Chairman of the Board may not be naturally visible to you, may not speak to you in an audible voice, and may not physically enforce His accountability. But one of humankind's most common and disastrous mistakes is thinking that just because God isn't seen, He's not present. Despite His invisibility, God is more real than any physical object you can see, touch, taste, hear, or smell. That day of accounting in which He reviews the results of our stewardship of His gifts is also quite real.

This represents one of the core challenges of being a human believer—navigating the fact that our most important relationship is with someone we can't see with our natural eyes. That's why the primary currency of the Christian life is *faith*. Faith perceives what we cannot see naturally. As Hebrews 11:1 reminds us, "Now faith is the substance of things hoped for, the evidence of things *not seen*" (emphasis added). This means that one of the core challenges of being a successful steward means remembering that you're accountable for the caretaking of what was entrusted to you by an invisible, intangible Owner.

> The primary currency of the Christian life is *faith*.

I'm a bit of a grammar nerd. I know that in the sentence "You are a steward," the word *steward* is a noun. Yet so far in this book I've also used that same word as a verb. As in, "I need to steward my resources well." And as we all know, verbs are action words. Now, you can be passive if you don't mind being a bad steward. But good stewardship requires action. We'll examine one of the most important actions you must take in the very next chapter. But for now, allow me to just remind you of what an extraordinary privilege it is to be entrusted with some things owned by the God and Creator of the universe.

My family is blessed to have a piece of ranch land that features some hills that rise above the horizon as you approach it. One day, as I spotted those hilltops, I started to frame the thought, *God, thank You for letting me own this land.* But even as the words formed in my mind, they hit a wall, and I could only think, *God, thank You for letting me steward this land!*

Steward. It works even better as a verb. Because you don't steward God's blessings by stuffing them into a box and burying them—you steward them by letting them live and breathe with you and by diligently and intentionally nurturing them into growth. It's an active process.

There's no getting around it. You are a CFO. Now let's roll up our sleeves and get to the nuts and bolts of what it takes to be a great one.

CHAPTER FIVE

FIRST THINGS FIRST

With high hopes and a knot in his stomach, Dave clicked open the email.

"Thank you for applying, but..."

He didn't need to read any further. This was clearly another in a long series of disappointing rejections by potential employers. His ongoing attempts to land a new and better job had proven fruitless and frustrating. His current job—working the night shift six or seven nights a week at a technology company—kept him from seeing much of his wife, Julie, and their two college-age kids. What was worse, the compensation wasn't great.

Julie, ever positive, had a gift for seeing the glass as half-full. It's what you might expect from a woman who had seen her daughter fight and ultimately beat neuroblastoma (a form of cancer found most commonly in infants) at a young age. Naturally frugal, Julie had demonstrated an uncanny ability to do a lot with just a little throughout their twenty-two years of marriage. With Dave's blessing, she served as the family finance manager, and she ran a tight ship. They both agreed they simply couldn't spend money on nonessentials like eating out, cable television, or mobile phones. Or tithing.

Around this time Dave and Julie (not their real names) became members of Gateway Church and began to hear me teaching about the power of putting God first in their finances.

"For a long time, I had been completely against tithing as a rule of thumb," Dave recalls. "It was like, if God needed the money, then He would have it. He doesn't need my money." The couple had been slowly chipping away at their debt for just over three years. However, they just couldn't seem to get the financial breakthrough they were working so hard to achieve. The family was at a low point, but all that was about to change.

One day on the way to work, Dave decided to listen to a CD of a sermon I titled "Jake's Motel." In it I share the story of how God transformed my life in an instant. He didn't know it, but Dave was about to experience the same thing. At the end of that message, I asked the congregation about their salvation. As Dave heard that question, he couldn't really say with certainty that he had experience new birth in Jesus Christ. "I couldn't say for certain that I was saved," Dave remembers. "So I dedicated my life to Christ right there in my car. I instantly felt a change and broke down in tears."

Over the next month, Dave was baptized, and the couple dove headlong into all Gateway had to offer. This included signing up for some of the spiritual development classes we offer periodically. The freshly energized couple wanted to learn as much as possible as quickly as possible. So they decided to divide and conquer. He attended one class and Julie attended our stewardship course.

After the first session, which covered the basics of stewardship, including tithing, Julie approached the instructor and explained their financial situation. He guided her to some of the very Scriptures we're about to examine, and assured her that if they would trust and honor God by returning to Him what is His, they would begin to see God working in their financial situation. Later that evening, Julie shared everything she'd heard with Dave.

In that moment, this couple stood at a significant point of decision. They were at a fork in the road. They had struggled financially throughout most of their two-plus decades of marriage. One road meant continuing to do things the same way they had been doing them in the past and hoping for better results. The other road involved a leap of faith. It meant doing something that didn't make total sense to their natural minds—that is, taking 10 percent of an income that was already stretched much farther than it could go and redirecting it to God via the church where they were being spiritually fed.

After praying together, Dave and Julie were in agreement. They already knew God was capable of doing miracles in the area of physical health—their daughter had been cancer-free for more than a decade. This encouraged them to step out and trust Him with their fiscal health. "We just need to knuckle down and start tithing," Dave remembers saying. And they did.

On their very next payday—Dave still recalls the exact date: February 28, 2013—Julie logged onto our church website and made their first-ever tithe as the very first expenditure of that pay period. God came first. They'd trust Him to help them work out the rest.

Less than twenty-four hours later, Dave was at his computer checking email again. This time there was a message from a company at which he hadn't even applied for a job. Somehow, the head of a local cable company had come across Dave's resume on an employment listing site. He was offering Dave a job! Not only were the hours much better, but the salary was more than Dave anticipated, and there were health benefits, too. With gratitude and faith, they continued their new lifestyle of putting God first in their finances.

Julie looks back now and says, "Immediately our finances made a complete turnaround." Today, other than their home mortgage, they are completely debt-free. In addition to paying off nearly $30,000 in personal debt, they watched a seemingly immovable mountain of hospital debt be uprooted and cast into the sea.

It's remarkable what will happen when an individual or a couple makes a firm decision to start putting God first. Speaking of first... that is the essence of the first commandment that God gave Moses to give to His people. Let's explore that concept further.

> It's remarkable what will happen when an individual or a couple makes a firm decision to start putting God first.

A Question of Priorities

First things first. It's a familiar cliché. It's also the title of a 1995 book by Stephen Covey on time management. In it, Covey, author of the mega–best seller *The 7 Habits of Highly Effective People,* offered advice and strategies for setting priorities in life. One of the key pieces of insight in the book is that, in our day-to-day lives, not everything that seems urgent is truly important. And not everything that is genuinely important feels urgent in the moment. In fact, he pointed out that often the most important things of all don't shout with urgency. They don't scream for attention. They just sit there quietly, being neglected or overlooked.

Covey pointed out that in our fast-paced, always-connected world, it's very easy to live our lives ruled by "the tyranny of the urgent." We can end up constantly rushing from crisis to crisis, fire to fire, and never addressing the nonurgent but vitally important things that will actually contribute to long-term success. As a result, we order our priorities all wrong. There is a lot of wisdom in that observation.

Perhaps that is why our gracious God went to so much trouble to help us prioritize things properly. To help us put "first things first."

He did it for Adam and Eve in the garden. He said clearly, "From any tree of the garden you may eat. Except *this* one. Leave this one alone. It's not for you. Enjoy all the others as blessings and gifts from me." All that very first human couple had to do was keep God first by leaving alone that which He said belonged to Him. Of course, we know how that story ends.

He again spoke clearly when He called out the Israelites from Egypt to be His covenant people. On Mount Sinai He gave Moses ten commandments to give to the people. He carved them Himself on tablets of stone. Do you recall what the first of those commandments was? In case it didn't come to you right away, the answer is, "You shall have no other gods before Me" (Exod. 20:3).

That's right. The very first commandment is God clearly saying that He must come first in our lives.

But in our day, it's so easy to shrug and assume that this commandment is only about Old Testament idolatry and therefore isn't relevant to us. You've probably never been tempted to construct a golden calf in your living room or build an altar to Baal on your patio. Nevertheless, I can assure you that idolatry is alive and well on planet earth. There are still many things vying for first place on your list of priorities. Our world is filled with attractive and enticing candidates for your worship and your sacrifice. It is with good reason that the apostle John closed his letter that we call the book of First John with these words:

Dear children, keep yourselves from idols. (5:21 NIV)

That was great advice then, and it is great advice now. There is simply no way around it. If you want to live a life beyond blessed, God must be first. This isn't for His benefit. It's for yours. And I'm not just talking about putting Him first in your finances—although that is certainly part of it. It means making Him a priority in every aspect of your life.

But how can you know if you're putting God first or if, rather, you are worshipping a false god—an idol? In other words, how can you know what it is you're truly worshipping? Here's a simple guide. What you worship is whatever provides your sense of identity. What you worship is what gives you a

> Whatever you seek out *first*—that's what you worship.

sense of security. It's where you run in a time of trouble. It's what you're most prone to give your time and attention to. Whatever you seek out *first*—that's what you worship.

The consistent witness of Scripture, from beginning to end, is that if our lives are going to be properly ordered and "blessable," God must be first. Why? Because He *is* first. Before anything else was, God was. He created everything, including you and me.

There is yet another way that God's Word helps us understand how to keep our priorities straight and keep God first. I'm talking about the biblical principle of *firstfruits*.

Honoring God as First by Bringing Him the First

When God delivered the Israelites out of slavery in Egypt, one of the first things He did was instruct them on how to be in relationship with Him. If you've ever participated in a plan or program to read through the Bible in a year, you may have found the passages in Leviticus and Numbers rough going. They do indeed contain a lot of detailed instruction that can be pretty challenging to slog through. I will admit they're generally not the most exciting parts of the Bible. Exodus is easier because at least stuff happens in Exodus!

Yet in all these books, we find something very important—God giving the people He loved keys to being His possession and to succeeding in the land of promise they were about to enter. And one of the most significant of these was the principle and practice of the firstfruits offering. This was an offering at harvest time in which the farmers would bring in to the priests of the Tabernacle offerings of the very first crops to have ripened. Twice—in Exodus 23:19 and 34:26—God, through Moses, establishes and commands the firstfruits offering, saying, "The first of the firstfruits of your land you shall bring into the house of the LORD your God."

Did you notice that it isn't just the firstfruits that God is to receive here, but rather the *first* of those firstfruits! As we're about to see, *first* things are so very important to God. That's why we see parallels to the principle of firstfruits in Scripture in the form of the principle of the firstborn and, of course, the tithe. All of these holy offerings and acts of worship are simply strands in the same cord of truth—that putting and keeping God first is the key to a life of fruitfulness in God's kingdom. It's everywhere.

For example, in the thirteenth chapter of Exodus, God is about to perform His great miracle of deliverance out of Egypt for the Israelites. On the night of the first Passover, God says,

> Consecrate to Me all the firstborn, whatever opens the womb among the children of Israel, both of man and beast; it is Mine. (Exodus 13:2)

Please notice that God plainly declares that the firstborn belongs to Him. "It is Mine," He said. This isn't the only time He does so. Sixteen times in Scripture God lays claim to the firstborn. Why is this such an important concept to God? Because it is the spiritual principle through which He ultimately redeemed us back to Himself! The only way to restore what Adam had forfeited and bring us back to an eternal life-giving connection to Himself was to offer up His innocent, spotless firstborn. Jesus was God's firstfruits offering.

I went into much greater depth concerning the wonderful meaning of the principle of firstfruits and the firstborn in my previous book, *The Blessed Life*, so I won't replicate all of that here. I recommend that you get it and read it, as it is very much the complementary companion to this book. (Remember, the blessed life walks on two legs!) For now, please just understand that the Bible couldn't be clearer about the need for us to put and keep God first in everything. There is enormous spiritual power and significance in it.

That means putting Him first in the management of our time, our relationships, and yes, our spending.

Firstfruits in Finances

Clearly, God must be first in every area of our lives, and that certainly includes the area of finances. Yet this is the very area in which so many people seem to struggle most. We have already seen one significant reason why.

The spirit of Mammon attaches itself to money and wants to be worshipped. And I just pointed out that whatever you allow to provide your identity and security is the true object of your worship. Untold millions look to money to provide both of those things. I also demonstrated that the true object of our worship is that to which we readily give time and attention. Again, few things in this world get more time or attention than financial matters. People obsess endlessly over the status of their bank balance, investment portfolios, or 401(k). Today, smartphones allow us to monitor the rises and falls of the world markets on a minute-by-minute basis.

For many of us, when we're not focusing on money, we're obsessing over the things money can buy. Glossy magazines, home remodeling shows on television, and internet sites feed us an endless stream of beautiful things to covet and crave—houses, cars, clothes, electronics, and trips.

Yes, Mammon wants your worship, but that worship belongs solely to God. So how do you put God first in your finances? The answer is simple yet seemingly so difficult for so many. The tithe.

The word *tithe* simply means "tenth," as in the fraction one-tenth. Just as God declared the firstborn of the Israelite's flocks to be His, and the first of the ripening harvest to be His, so He also declares the tithe to be His as well. Of course, most of us don't earn our living through farming anymore. And even farmers convert their crops to cash these days rather than storing them in barns. That means your tithe/firstfruits offering will almost always be in the form of money. And the biblical principle is to give a tithe of your "increase":

> Honor the LORD with your possessions,
>> and with *the firstfruits of all your increase*;
>> so your barns will be filled with plenty,
>> and your vats will overflow with new wine. (Proverbs 3:9–
> 10, emphasis added)

First. Firstborn. Firstfruits. We see this heavenly pattern for worship repeated throughout Scripture. Why? Is it because God is greedy or needy? Is He insecure or demanding? Why would a God who owns everything ask you for 10 percent of your income each pay period?

The answer is that God is not really interested in your money. He's interested in your heart. The things of God always come down to the status and motivations of your heart. He wants to help you keep your heart set and focused on Him because that's the only way you can experience all the goodness in this life that He wants you to experience and, more importantly, make the largest eternal impact for His kingdom.

> God is not really interested in your money. He's interested in your heart.

Tithing isn't legalism. It's life. Spiritual life. It's hard to overemphasize this. The stewardship practice of faithfully tithing is neither *for* Him nor *about* Him. It's for *you*. About *you*. This is why, although some accurately call this the principle of tithing, I like to call it the principle of putting God first.

The tithe exists as both a reminder and test. It's a reminder that God actually owns it all. And it's a test of whether or not God is truly in the *first*-place position in your life. It's also a test because it takes faith and trust in the goodness and faithfulness of God to return His 10 percent to Him first before you start addressing your other physical needs. There is no faith involved if you wait until all your other bills are paid to return God's tithe to Him. What does it say about our priorities when we diligently pay everybody else first and then see if there is enough leftover to give God His portion?

Yet the tithe is much more than a test. It's actually a spiritual gateway for God to enter your circumstances and place His blessing on the remaining 90 percent of your income. This stems from the little-understood spiritual principle that a firstfruits offering to God redeems all of the remaining portion. The first bit, as it is offered, carries the power to redeem the rest. This is the essence of Paul's message in Romans 11:16:

> For if the firstfruit is holy, the lump is also holy; and if the root is holy, so are the branches.

This is so important for you. In trying to navigate the current chaotic, volatile, uncertain financial seas, which would you rather have: (*a*) 100 percent of your income with no blessing on it, or (*b*) 90 percent of your income with God's wholehearted supernatural blessing on it? Let me tell you that I and many others have tried it both ways, and every faithful tither will tell you that option *b* is much better! Time and again I've seen the redeemed 90 percent stretch miraculously far—not unlike that little boy's lunch that fed thousands after Jesus blessed it (Mark 6:30–44). I've also repeatedly seen an unredeemed 100 percent get eaten up by unexpected expenses and repairs almost before it hit the bank account.

The first portion is the portion that redeems the rest. (Again, you'll find a deeper exploration of this powerful spiritual principle in *The Blessed Life*.) The first portion carries the blessing. That's why you don't want to give the first portion to the mortgage company, the finance company, or the cable provider. Those entities carry no power to redeem and bless your remaining funds. Unfortunately, it seems that many Christians revere the IRS and the mortgage company more than they revere God. The principle of putting God first says, "Yes, I have a stack of bills here, but I'm going to give to God first and trust Him to bless the rest of my 'lump' of income."

Your Bible is literally saturated with this concept. We've already seen it in Proverbs 3:9–10 wherein the wise Solomon advises us to honor the Lord from the first of all our increase. We also see it in Genesis where God accepted Abel's offering because it represented his first, but not Cain's because it wasn't his first (Genesis 4). We see it in the Israelites' conquest of Canaan, when God declares Jericho—the first city they conquered—His (Joshua 6). They were solemnly commanded not to touch any of the spoils of that city when it fell. We see it as God asks Abraham for Isaac because he was his firstborn (Genesis 22). But this principle isn't isolated to the Old Testament.

We find it in Jesus' Sermon on the Mount. There Jesus tells His disciples to "seek first the kingdom of God and his righteousness, and all these things shall be added to you" (Matt. 6:33). Notice the placement of *first*. The larger context of Jesus' statement is our very real need for food, clothing, and shelter. Here, Jesus Himself assures us that if we put God first, we can be confident that God will take care of those material needs.

Yes, it's just stuff. But if you won't put God first when it comes to mere stuff, it is revealing a much deeper issue in your heart. It's very possible the spirit of Mammon is entrenched and rooted there. Tithing will shatter that hold.

There is a wonderful and vivid illustration of this truth in the Old Testament book of I Kings. Do you remember the story of Elijah and the widow in I Kings 17?

During a time of drought and famine in Israel, Elijah had been living in the wilderness. For a period of time he experienced miraculous provision there. He had water from a stream that somehow hadn't dried up. And each day ravens brought him food. Eventually, however, the stream gradually dried up. At that same time, the ravens stopped coming. Elijah knew this was a sign that God wanted him to relocate. In fact, God told Elijah to move to the city of Zarephath, where He had instructed a widow there to provide for him.

As Elijah approached the gate of that city, he spotted a woman gathering firewood. He wondered if this was the widow God had mentioned, so he gave her a little test. He asked her to bring him a little water in a cup. Remember, this is in the midst of a severe drought, so water is precious. What's more, the person making the request was a stranger to her. Nevertheless, she immediately agreed and started to do as he asked, but as she was leaving, he called out an additional request. I'm paraphrasing, but Elijah basically said, "Oh, and can you bring me a piece of bread while you're at it?"

She turns back to the prophet and says, "As the LORD your God lives, I do not have bread, only a handful of flour in a bin, and a little oil in a jar; and see, I am gathering a couple of sticks that I may go in and prepare it for myself and my son, that we may eat it, and die" (I Kings 17:12). In other words, she told Elijah that he'd interrupted her in the process of preparing *her last meal* for her and her son. Starvation waited on the other side of this final, simple little dinner.

This grim revelation didn't seem to faze Elijah one bit. He replied, "Don't be afraid! Go ahead and do just what you've said, but make a little bread for me *first*. Then use what's left to prepare a meal for yourself and your son. For this is what the LORD, the God of Israel, says: There will always be flour and olive oil left in your containers until the time when the LORD sends rain and the crops grow again!" (NLT, emphasis added).

This widow stepped out in faith and gave to the man of God first. And God miraculously blessed the rest of her meager supply. Do you know how long it was until the Lord sent rain? Three years and six months! In all that time, the flour wasn't used up and the oil didn't run dry.

Why? Because she gave to God first.

Climb into her shoes (or sandals), and you'll see how easy it would have been for her to rationalize saying no to Elijah's request. She must have thought, "Elijah has been out there in the desert sun too long! I just have enough for one more meal—yet this joker wants some of it. And he wants his *first*. Elijah is crazy!"

Sometimes, when I'm teaching about giving the first 10 percent of your income to God, I can feel some of the people sitting and listening to me—good people, people who love God but can't pay their bills—thinking the very same thing about me. "Pastor Robert must be out of his mind. I can't even pay my bills or support my family, and he wants me to give ten percent, off the top, to the invisible Creator of the Universe through my local church?"

If that would describe you, then this story poses a fascinating question for you. Why, in the midst of a drought and famine, would

God send His very own prophet to an impoverished widow? Don't you think God could have sent Elijah to a rich man in Zarephath who could have helped out Elijah far more easily and painlessly? Why send him to a widowed mother on the brink of starvation?

I believe there's a simple and powerful reason.

> God did not send Elijah to the widow to provide for Elijah—He sent Elijah to provide for the widow.

God did not send Elijah to the widow to provide for Elijah—He sent Elijah to provide for the widow.

Again, tithing is not for God's benefit; it's for ours. He had already sent ravens to feed Elijah, and He certainly could have continued to do so. For that matter, He could have sent an angel from heaven to make him a cake—the first Angel Food Cake. (Sorry—I couldn't resist.)

So why instead choose such an awkward and inefficient source of help? Because there was a widow who needed to be provided for—who was going to die. As we've already noted, the plight of widows and orphans holds a very special place in God's heart. God cared so deeply about her that he sent a man of God to answer her prayers. But God knew that far more than bread or even hope, this woman needed a properly aligned relationship with Himself. So He sent a man of God who said to her, "Give to me first. Give to God first—then watch what happens to your provisions." He sent someone to test her willingness to put God first even when it hurt. (And notice, by the way, that she was fully aware of who Elijah was and who he represented, as shown by her oath to "the LORD your God." She knew this was no random crackpot wandering up on the street. This was a fair test of her faith in the God of Israel.

Again, God did not send Elijah to the widow to provide for

Elijah—He sent Elijah to the widow because He cared about her. But there is no getting around the spiritual principle of firstfruits. To get the blessing of multiplication on her tiny reserve of oil and flour, she needed to take some of it and give it to God...*first*. Only then could the rest of the "lump" be blessed.

By the way, this was not only about finances—just as your tithes don't only affect your money. It's also about our loved ones. If you read further into the story, you learn that later on the widow's son gets sick and dies—and Elijah raises him from the dead. Do you think that God knew that her son was going to get sick? Of course He did. He knows the future. He sent Elijah there not only to provide for her, but also to bless her. She'd already lost her husband. Now her only son—the one who would care for her in her old age—was about to get sick and die. So God sent a man of God into her life.

However, all of the blessing and provision hinged upon her being willing to respect the principle of putting God first.

What About You?

Let me ask you something. What if God came to you in person, like He appeared to Abraham and Moses, and said to you, "If you will tithe—if you will give me the first ten percent of your income—I will do two things for you. First, I will stand at the door of your house and keep the devil out. I will keep him out of your marriage, keep him away from your teenage kids, and keep him out of your health. Secondly, I will bless you so that you actually have more than what you're currently making"?

If He showed up, in all His glory, and promised you that

face-to-face, would you take Him at His word and give Him the first tenth of your increase? Well, He's done just short of that very thing. In His holy, infallible Word, God says this:

"Bring the whole tithe into the storehouse, so that there may be food in My house, and test Me now in this," says the LORD of hosts, "if I will not open for you the windows of heaven and pour out for you a blessing until it overflows. Then I will rebuke the devourer for you, so that it will not destroy the fruits of the ground; nor will your vine in the field cast its grapes," says the LORD of hosts. (Malachi 3:10–11 NASB)

Wouldn't you be foolish not to accept that deal? What rational person would say no to that offer? Yet millions upon millions of believers say no to it month after month.

Dear reader, the fact that you've stuck with me so far in this book reveals that you truly want to apply biblical wisdom in your finances and experience a life beyond blessed. Well, there is no key more vital or more impactful than this one. God must be first. And when you put Him first in your finances by devoting the first tenth of all your increase to Him, something remarkable and significant happens in your heart.

> When you put Him first in your finances by devoting the first tenth of all your increase to Him, something remarkable and significant happens.

What's more, in doing so you activate the spiritual principle of firstfruits, opening up a gateway of access for God to redeem and work and bless and multiply throughout every area of your life.

First things first.

CHAPTER SIX

HUMBLY GRATEFUL, NOT GRUMBLY HATEFUL

For a moment, Andy wasn't sure whether he had just gotten off a Boeing 747 or an interstellar spaceship. He was definitely tempted to wonder if he had just landed on an alien planet.

In reality, Andy, a longtime member of Gateway Church, had just arrived in Luanda, the capital of Angola, as a volunteer with a team from James Robison's ministry, Life Outreach International (LOI). They were there to document LOI's ongoing efforts to save the lives of malnourished children in one of the poorest nations on earth. After nearly twenty-four straight hours of nonstop travel, the group had stumbled out of the plane, into a shuttle bus, and now found themselves at the hotel where they would spend the night, before heading out into rural Angola the following morning.

This can't possibly be where we're staying, Andy thought to himself as he stood in front of the hotel with his duffel bag in hand and backpack over his shoulder.

Compounding the jet lag was a disorienting assault on all five of his senses. Visually, the street looked like something out of a postapocalyptic movie. Abandoned cars covered in a thick blanket of gray-brown dirt lined the unpaved, trash-littered street. Graffiti covered many of the cars and buildings. Gaunt, mangy stray dogs wandered amid the garbage as a few clusters of Angolan men eyed the group and conversed in a language he didn't understand. But it was the smell that really hit him hard. His watering eyes, scanning for the source, quickly identified it. A ditch running the length of the street directly in front of the hotel was an open sewer. The hotel itself looked equally grim.

Andy was an invited guest on this trip and wasn't about to question or complain. He knew it wasn't a resort vacation he'd signed up for. And he ultimately learned that this was actually a rather expensive hotel, even by US standards. Years of civil war and Marxist governance have made Luanda one of the most expensive cities on earth in which to live or visit. LOI, ever conscious of the need to be frugal with donated funds, had spent the bare minimum necessary on the hotel rooms, yet the cost of one night in this hotel would have purchased a nice room in a Hyatt or Hilton in any major American city. Andy shuddered to think what a "cheap" hotel there would be like.

The following day the team packed up and headed south out of the capital city to a spot in the rural heart of the nation—an area that would be their base of operation for the next week as they checked in on what the ministry's partners were doing through several malnutrition clinics. Camping was like a picnic compared to Luanda. Nevertheless, nothing could have prepared Andy for what he encountered at those clinics. Angola perennially has one of the highest infant mortality rates in the world, and the clinics there were swamped with desperate mothers who had, in many cases, walked for days to bring their heartbreakingly weak infants to the clinic. Compounding the shock was the fact that these mothers often waited until their babies' situations were critical before even beginning the journey.

As a result, Andy saw poverty-driven heartache, suffering, and misery everywhere he looked in this place. A seemingly endless stream of skeletal infants and toddlers barely clinging to life, and their heartsick mothers, filled each day. He visited village after village where clean water was nonexistent and the communal bathroom for the entire community was simply a spot in a patch of dirt with borders marked by twine. All of this would have been jarring and disorienting at any time for any person not accustomed to seeing desperate need. But for Andy, the trip was doubly impactful because of the battle that had recently been taking place in his heart back home.

You see, Andy lived in a modest, working-class Fort Worth suburb; had a nice little house in a quiet, friendly neighborhood; two good, reliable cars that were paid for, free and clear; enjoyed date nights with his wife at good restaurants a couple of times each month; and every three or four years they took a nice vacation trip. Yet for some time now, he had increasingly begun to feel short-changed by life and by God. A slow but steady drip of toxic bitterness had been seeping into his heart, and he wasn't even really aware of it.

The problem is that Andy's suburb just happened to be adjacent to two of the most affluent zip codes in all of Texas. What's more, his daily commute took him through one of those upscale communities and into the heart of the other one. His daily drive took him past dozens of walled, gated neighborhoods filled with spectacular homes. Driving by the enormous houses with manicured lawns each day, he'd ask himself, *What do these people do? Where exactly does all this money come from?*

At lunch each day, the streets around his office seemed to be a parade of high-end luxury automobiles. It wasn't just that most cars seemed to carry brand names like Mercedes, Lexus, BMW, Jaguar, Porsche, and Audi. Those were the guys who were "slumming" it in this part of town. With increasing frequency, he was seeing Lamborghinis, Maseratis, and Bentleys, too. These were cars that cost as much as or more than his house! With each passing day, Andy had begun to feel that his plain, dependable six-year-old vehicle was nothing more than a rolling advertisement that he wasn't doing as well as everyone else.

Of course, he knew at some intellectual level that what he was witnessing wasn't average or normal, even in prosperous America. Even so, immersed in this on a daily basis—on top of the steady stream to his smartphone of social media feeds that made everyone else's lives look fun and fabulous—Andy had been feeling increasingly resentful and miserable. He'd begun to hate his house, his neighborhood, his car...his life.

He wanted more. He wanted better. He felt he *deserved* more and better. Without realizing it, Andy had slowly, incrementally become a walking bundle of envy, resentment, dissatisfaction, and discontent. Almost imperceptibly, his life had become grim and joyless as he began devoting rising levels of time and attention to ways he could make more money or, at minimum, *look* like he made more. Somewhere along the way he had lost any sense of gratitude for the long list of good things in his life. These included a great relationship with his wife; grown children who were all saved, serving God, and doing well in life; robust health; and a circle of close friends who loved and respected him.

Then he somehow found himself in Angola and found his entire perspective on his life getting a massive, jarring recalibration. Suddenly he was seeing his lifestyle through a very different lens.

The clincher came on one of his final days in Africa. He was standing under a shade tree on the edge of a tiny, remote village in the heart of the country. In that quiet moment he spotted a gangly, young, barefoot boy of about eight years of age galloping by at full speed. The child had a stick about two feet long and was using it to roll a rusty old rim from a bicycle wheel, keeping the metal ring rolling in front of him as he ran. *This is what this poor kid has for a toy,* he thought to himself, feeling a fresh surge of pity for the people of that place. Then he caught a glimpse of the boy's face. It held an expression of pure delight. Joy. Freedom.

In that moment the Spirit of God arrested Andy's heart in a fresh and powerful way. A wave of deep repentance washed over him like an ocean wave.

God in heaven, I'm so sorry. How ungrateful I've been!

That image, along with many less happy ones, burned itself into Andy's memory in that life-changing week. On more than one occasion in the days after returning home, Andy repeated a solemn vow to God: "Lord, I can't believe how great my life is. I'll never complain about my circumstances again. Thank you!" Little in his day-to-day life had changed, yet his enjoyment of it and, most importantly, his joy in his relationship with God returned at a higher level than ever before.

Andy discovered the enormous power of the simple heart of gratitude. I want to help you discover that power, too. It's far more important than you can imagine. Let's dive in and I'll explain why.

> There is enormous power of the simple heart of gratitude.

An Epidemic of Ingratitude

We're living in angry times. Have you noticed? Everyone seems on edge. Irritable. Resentful and short. And it's not just when we're on the freeways in traffic. Yes, the internet has a lot to do with it. As a nation we're polarized like never before. But it runs deeper than that. I think a root cause of our current climate of anger is unthankfulness—along with its constant companions: envy, resentment, and discontent. The Bible actually validates that idea.

> Where do wars and fights come from among you? Do they not come from your desires for pleasure that war in your members? You lust and do not have. You murder and covet and cannot obtain. You fight and war. Yet you do not have because you do not ask. You ask and do not receive, because you ask amiss, that you may spend it on your pleasures. (James 4:1–3)

When we allow an ungrateful heart to develop within us, we find ourselves angry at everyone and everything around us. Ingratitude for the blessings we have causes us to view the blessings of others with resentment rather than being genuinely happy for them. What's worse, that unthankful heart actually cuts us off from the additional goodness God wants to bring into our lives. Materialism and the spirit of Mammon have permeated our culture, and as they have, ingratitude, discontent, and anger have risen accordingly.

Be thankful for the standard of living God has provided for you.

A major key to successful stewardship and a life of blessing is simply maintaining a grateful heart. In other words, be thankful for the standard of living God has provided for you. So many Scriptures point us in that direction. For example, 1 Thessalonians 5:18 says, "In everything give thanks; for this is the will of God in Christ Jesus for you." It doesn't get much clearer than that. God's will is for you to maintain a thankful posture in every circumstance. Psalm 100 says that gratitude and thankfulness need to be a central part of our approach to God's throne:

> Enter into his gates with thanksgiving, and into his courts with praise: be thankful unto him, and bless his name. (v. 4 KJV)

The fact is that we always have so much for which to be grateful to God. Yet you would not know this to listen to the typical American Christian in the typical American church. We're living better than four-fifths of the world and yet we're unthankful for the standard of living God has provided for us. The typical working-class American enjoys a lifestyle the medieval kings of Europe would have envied. There has never been a better time on planet earth to be alive. Yet so many of God's people are living like Andy before God snapped him out of his fog of ingratitude and discontent in Angola. They're so busy coveting what others have, and aware of what they *don't* have, that they completely lose sight of all God has done for them.

That's why so many are attracted to a "prosperity gospel" message that assures them they not only *can* have more and better of everything, but *should* have more and better of everything. Now, please don't misunderstand. There is nothing wrong with having a nicer house or driving a nice car. We've already seen what a pitfall the poverty mind-set is for faithful stewards. God rewards good stewards with more to steward. My point is that a heart for faithful stewardship begins by being genuinely thankful for the lifestyle and standard of living you have *now*.

Close the Door

Please understand: Chronic ingratitude opens the door to all kinds of evil in your life. This is such an important truth. Unthankfulness toward God literally opens a door to the enemy in your life—one through which he can bring a whole litany of bad things.

> Chronic ingratitude opens the door to all kinds of evil in your life.

Would you like to see scriptural evidence for that? You'll find it in the first chapter of Romans, where Paul writes,

> Because, although they knew God, they did not glorify Him as God, *nor were thankful*, but became futile in their thoughts, and their foolish hearts were darkened. Professing to be wise, they became fools, and changed the glory of the incorruptible God into an image made like corruptible man—and birds and four-footed animals and creeping things.
>
> Therefore God also gave them up to uncleanness, in the lusts of their hearts, to dishonor their bodies among themselves, who exchanged the truth of God for the lie, and worshiped and served the creature rather than the Creator, who is blessed forever. Amen. (Romans 1:21–25, emphasis added)

Paul is talking about a group of people who began simply being ungrateful to God and refusing to recognize Him in His goodness. But the picture Paul paints is of a steady downward slide from there. For example, when he says, "Their foolish hearts were darkened," he means they moved into great deception. This deception led to gross idolatry and, if you read the rest of the chapter, even more depravity and a list of virtually every imaginable kind of wickedness and evil. Yet it all started with plain, old ingratitude.

Ingratitude to God is also on another list of horrible things, this one made by Paul in his letter to Timothy. In 2 Timothy 3:1–5, Paul writes,

> But know this, that in the last days perilous times will come: For men will be lovers of themselves, lovers of money, boasters, proud, blasphemers, disobedient to parents, *unthankful*, unholy, unloving, unforgiving, slanderers, without self-control, brutal, despisers of good, traitors, headstrong, haughty, lovers of pleasure rather than lovers of God, having a form of godliness but denying its power. And from such people turn away! (emphasis added)

Let me say this again: Unthankfulness opens the door to all kinds of evil in our lives. When we allow the enemy to begin to subtly, gradually, insidiously maneuver us into a place where we are not thankful for what God has provided, we're in a vulnerable place.

Putting the Blame Where It Belongs

We have a tempting opportunity to slip into unthankfulness whenever we feel like our needs aren't being met. If a person's outgo is consistently more than his or her income, it's deceptively easy to start pointing an accusing finger at God. I know because I've been there.

I talk to Christians all the time who clearly feel confused, wounded, neglected, or even betrayed because they believe God is not delivering on His commitment to provide for them. They point to Jesus' words in Matthew 6 where He tells His disciples, "Therefore do not worry, saying, 'What shall we eat?' or 'What shall we drink?' or 'What shall we wear?' For after all these things the Gentiles seek. For your heavenly Father knows that you need all these things" (vv. 31–32). They look at their monthly shortfall and conclude God is not holding up His end. That's really the way they feel.

It can be a very hard fact to see and embrace, but the root of the problem in these situations isn't God's level of provision. It's our mismanagement of what He has provided. We mismanage the funds that God gave us, and then we get mad at Him for not covering and compensating for our mismanagement.

How do I know this? Because years ago, I was in that very same place. I was deep in debt and could not pay my bills. I vividly remember saying, "God, I don't understand. I see you providing for others but you're not providing for me. Look at this. I can't pay my bills!" Would you like to know what our God kindly and patiently said to me in reply? He said, "Robert, I'm not responsible for bills I didn't tell you to incur. I'm not responsible for debts that I didn't tell you to take on. You signed your name on that note without talking to me about it. I didn't sign my name on it."

It's not that God wasn't willing to help Debbie and me put our finances in order. His point was that He wasn't going to bless my doing my own thing. He wasn't going to cover my foolishness with His resources. I had been asking God to fund and facilitate *my* plan.

God was saying, "Take the hard steps necessary to live within the income I'm providing for you now. Then watch what I do."

That's precisely what we did. Of course, we did not get into that dire situation overnight and we didn't get out of it overnight, either. It took Debbie and me several years to get our finances in order after we began applying the principles I'm describing in this book. Let me tell you what *did* happen overnight, though. Peace and joy flooded back into our home. When we set our hearts to be thankful for and content with what we had, rather than buying everything our hearts desired,

> When we set our hearts to be thankful for and content with what we had, rather than buying everything our hearts desired, the atmosphere in our home and marriage improved immediately.

the atmosphere in our home and marriage improved immediately.

As I said, it took a while to get out of the mess we were in. We owed a lot of money. If you're in a mess, it will take some time for you, too. But you don't have to wait to experience the joy and peace that come with being thankful.

Take Your Medicine

When Debbie and I finally got serious about giving God complete control of our finances, one of the things God said to me was, "Your big monthly car payment has to go. Stop financing things you can't afford."

That directive was no small thing. I'm embarrassed now to tell you, but at that time we carried a monthly car payment that was bigger than our monthly house payment! That's right—we were paying more for a rapidly depreciating car each month than to keep a roof over our heads. Looking back on it now, it seems ridiculous to me, but it's true nonetheless. How did that happen? I rationalized it—that's how. My flesh wanted that shiny new thing, so my mind found a way to sign off on the decision as being a great idea. (Be honest—you do it, too!) Our carnal minds have an amazing power to rationalize buying ourselves things that we really want as being good, godly, and prudent.

I had purchased it assuming that God would endorse and enable my poor stewardship by increasing our income enough to make it all work out financially. He didn't. Instead—once I started listening to Him with a humble, open heart—He said, "Sell that car."

God didn't seem to be aware of the realities of car depreciation, so I graciously volunteered to illuminate Him. "God, I owe more on that car than I can get for it by selling it. I'm upside down on it!" I heard Him say in reply, "Yes, son, you're more upside down right now than you know." It was hard to hear but true. I had a lot of things inverted where my handling of our finances was concerned.

"Lord, if I sell it, I'll lose money," I persisted. Looking back on it now, what an ironic line of argument to offer. I was basically saying it would be a bad financial decision to sell the car at a loss. The guy who had willingly signed up for a car payment bigger than his house payment and now couldn't pay his bills was resisting a directive from the God of the universe because it wouldn't be economically prudent or savvy. Oh, what a patient Father we have!

I'm not sure what I expected God to say in response to my lame protest. Perhaps something like, "Oh, you'll lose money on the sale? Golly, I didn't know that! Well, by all means, then—keep the car. I wouldn't want you to take a loss!" Not surprisingly, that's *not* what He said. His loving but firm reply was, "Get your finances in order, son."

So we sold the car. As I anticipated, we still owed several hundred dollars to the finance company after the sale. However, we had somehow managed to scrape together a little bit of savings in this season. We used a chunk of it to finish paying off the note on the car and had precisely $750 leftover. "What now, Lord?" we asked. "We need a car. Is this $750 our down payment for a less expensive car?" His reply stunned me. He said, "No, I want you to pay cash. Use the $750 to buy a car." At this point Debbie and I were fully committed to following God in our finances, so we took a deep breath and said, "Okay, Lord. Help us find the $750 car you want us to have."

Not surprisingly, there weren't a lot of them to choose from. I felt prompted by the Lord to tell a friend of mine what we were trying to do in being obedient to God in our finances. He recalled that he had a friend with an old station wagon sitting in his garage gathering dust that he had talked about possibly selling at some point. He called him and asked if he would sell it for $750, and after some thought, he agreed.

We found ourselves the grateful owners of a 1973 Ford station wagon with 134,000 miles on it. If you have read my earlier book, *The Blessed Life*, you may remember that in the opening paragraphs of the first chapter, I tell a story about rolling up to a mom-and-pop filling station in a "highly experienced" station wagon. Well, this was that vehicle. And I can honestly tell you that we loved that car. It wasn't much to look at. It certainly didn't impress anybody (as if impressing people matters one bit in the eternal scope of things). Yet every time we got in it, we felt such peace and joy. Those positive emotions stemmed from a combination of knowing we owned it free and clear and, more significantly, that we had obeyed God in buying it. Every time we got in it, we thanked God for it. We loved it. We prayed over it. We anointed it with oil (about a quart a week)!

We rejoiced in it because we knew we'd put ourselves in a position for God to begin to bless us. But the car was just part of a broader stewardship commitment. We decided we would not buy anything that was not an absolute necessity until we were out of debt. That meant we didn't go to the movies. We didn't go out to eat. We bargain shopped and clipped coupons for the necessities. We prayed about every significant expenditure. In other words, we got serious.

When you get truly serious about getting your finances in order, God gets serious about helping you. His enabling grace and power flow in your direction. I vividly recall one little example of this truth we experienced in that season.

> When you get truly serious about getting your finances in order, God gets serious about helping you.

Our handheld hair dryer died. Now remember, we had made a solemn vow to only purchase absolute necessities. Well, as all women and many men will understand, Debbie put a functioning hair dryer in the "necessity" category. I didn't disagree. I used it, too. But I said, "Honey, I'm with you. But let's pray about it first." When I asked God about it, I clearly heard the Lord say, "Wait one day." That was it. No elaboration or explanation. Just, "Wait one day." So I went back to Debbie and told her what I thought the Lord had said. My sweet wife, who has always trusted in my ability to hear the voice of the Lord, said, "Okay!" That was on a Saturday.

The next morning, we got up and went to church. For obvious

reasons, I don't think either one of us washed our hair that morning before getting ready. At church, a lady neither one of us could recall ever having met before walked up to us and said, "Excuse me. I was at Walmart yesterday and while I was there, I felt like God told me to buy you a hair dryer. I hope that's okay." Of course it was okay!

It was a small thing, but it spoke volumes to us about God's willingness and ability to meet our obedience with His power and love. I really want you to understand what I'm about to say. In *The Blessed Life*, I gave numerous examples about how God supernaturally blesses us when we become generous givers. What I am about to say is the core truth I want you to take away from this book. When we begin to set our finances in order, God supernaturally blesses us! It's more than just the numbers in the budget adding up mathematically. God begins to bless our "fish and loaves" as Jesus did when He fed the multitudes! Please don't miss this! God blesses good stewardship in the same way that He blesses generous giving!

Cultivate a Thankful Heart

Dear reader, I know the misery you go through when your finances are out of control. I've been there. It can crush you under a relentless, discouraging weight of pressure. That's why it's so very important to cultivate and maintain a heart of gratitude for what you have *now*. How do you do that?

One of the most powerful things you can do when you are discouraged, depressed, or under attack is to simply begin to thank God for what you have in your life. There is never a time in which a believer doesn't have much for which to be grateful. Relationships. Health. Meaningful work. A standard of living most people in the

> There is never a time in which a believer doesn't have much for which to be grateful.

world would consider opulent luxury. And of course, the overwhelmingly wonderful privilege of being a child of God who has an eternity in heaven waiting in the future.

You don't have to travel to the poorest villages of a third-world nation to readjust your level of contentment. Start thanking God now for the standard of living He has provided for you. Discontentment will move you to make foolish financial decisions. You'll spend money you don't have to buy things you don't need.

Inside every faithful steward beats a heart of gratitude.

CHAPTER SEVEN

HAPPY HEART, HAPPY HOME

While both in their midtwenties, Jack and Karen had started married life as most couples do—crazy in love and full of hope. They'd also started it deeply in debt.

Student loans made up most, but not all, of the debt burden the two had brought into their union. Both had used loans to finance their undergraduate degrees. They'd done the same thing to earn master's degrees as well. In fact, it was in grad school that they'd first met. Once out of school, both had rewarded themselves for their years of hard work and self-denial by leasing nice cars. Both had accumulated some credit card debt, as well. Even as repayment of student loans siphoned off a huge chunk of their individual earnings.

Once married the couple was carrying a staggering combined debt load of more than $400,000 on a total household income of less than $100,000. Of course, two can indeed live cheaper than one, but not *that* much cheaper. As a result, Jack and Karen quickly found the relentless financial pressure crushing the joy out of their lives and peace from their newly established home. What should have been some of the most carefree and exciting years of their lives together became a grim, losing battle to juggle obligations. They'd wanted to travel some before kids came along, but financial pressure had not only pushed travel out of the picture, it had pushed the prospect of having a baby out as well.

Their dreams of buying a house and starting a family seemed hopelessly out of reach. What's more, the constant tension was taking a toll on their relationship. They had never argued when they were dating, but soon it seemed all they did was fight. And more often than not those arguments were either directly or indirectly about money.

On the plus side, they shared a common faith and common values. They were believers and both desired to tithe and be generous to others. They made sure they did the former, but there was no money available to do the latter. They represented a textbook case for why I wrote this book. They desired to live a lifestyle of generosity but money management mistakes—past and present—made that impossible. And the poison fruit of those mistakes had turned their home and relationship toxic.

Mismanagement Misery

Every human being on earth is born broken. Flawed. With a selfish sin nature and desperately in need of redemption. As a result, every marriage is an exercise in getting *two* such people to live together in harmony for the rest of their lives. Maybe it's not a huge surprise that marriage isn't the easiest thing in the world to do successfully. Relationships don't need any more pressure than this fallen world (and our fallen natures) naturally put on them. Yet poor steward-ship adds to this pressure in huge, manifold ways.

In my experience, mismanagement of finances causes more marital problems than any other cause. I know this runs counter to some of the conventional wisdom about marriage. I've seen studies in the past that indicated that communication issues were actually the top source of problems in the home. But I think those studies are masking the root issue in many cases. A lot of broken, angry, hurtful, accusatory communication in marriage stems from the stress of financial pressure.

Yes, mismanagement of finances causes relational problems, but it takes a heavy toll in other areas as well. For example, the same stress that poisons communication in the home can cause a host of physical problems. And those physical problems result in additional medical expenses and lost income through missed days at work—a double whammy.

For some, like Jack and Karen, it's college loans that initiate the escalating spiral of financial pressure and misery. For many others, it comes from a different source—an insidious and devious decep-tion that is widespread in our culture. In fact, it is one of the spirit of Mammon's most successful lies.

The Seductive Lie

Years ago, I preached a sermon series titled The Ten Financial Com-mandments. The second in this series was, "Thou Shalt Not Try to Acquire Happiness Through Material Things." It was a financial parallel to the actual second commandment God delivered through Moses, "You shall not make for yourself a carved image" (Exod. 20:4).

Both commandments—mine and the one Moses received—are about idolatry. God is saying, "Don't look to anything on this earth for happiness. Don't look to anything on this earth for fulfillment."

The spirit of Mammon's most effective and seductive lie is that more money or more stuff will make you happy. When you *buy in* (literally) to that deception, you start purchasing things you can't afford in a never-ending quest to reach the carrot dangling on the end of the stick just beyond your nose. It remains forever and always tantalizingly just out of reach. *I hate everything hanging in my closet. If we just had a bigger house in a better neighborhood, I'd be content. If I just had a newer car, I'd be satisfied.* And here's the biggest, most disastrous lie of them all: *If I had a different spouse, I'd be happy.*

> The spirit of Mammon's most effective and seductive lie is that more money or more stuff will make you happy.

It's a lie. Once those cravings are achieved, the same old, familiar dissatisfaction quickly returns. Part of the trap is that no matter what level of stuff-accumulation you achieve, you look around and see people who have more or better. As I pointed out in the opening of this book, many very wealthy people are utterly miserable. And some people of very modest means live with contentment and great joy. My point is it's not the presence or absence of material possessions or wealth that determines happiness. But thinking that they do is a form of idolatry. And idolatry always leads to catastrophe.

Both rich and poor people fall into this trap. Mammon is an equal-opportunity destroyer.

Often when Christians are under the influence of this form of deception, they will try to sanctify their cravings by praying for and asking God to give them the object of their desire. They will even use the name of Jesus as some sort of mystical, magic phrase. To be honest, I view this as nothing more than the Church age version of "taking the Lord's name in vain"—the very thing God forbids in the third commandment.

How many times have you set your heart on a material thing so completely that it became a central focus of your life? I know I have. And I've watched others do the same thing. Desire is a powerful thing. Actually, it's something more powerful than mere desire. It's lust. The lust of the flesh, the lust of the eyes, and the boastful pride of life (I John 2:16).

This force carries such power to affect your behavior that some people in the worlds of professional sales, multilevel marketing, and success motivation have learned to use this phenomenon to get people to attain higher levels of achievement. Some coaches, sponsors, and sales managers will encourage someone to form an obsession with a material possession—perhaps a dream car, a boat, or a vacation home—in order to keep them focused, motivated, and ignoring rejection. They coach people to identify a thing they want desperately and then to keep it in front of them all the time. Let's say you've always thought it would be cool to have a high-end luxury boat. You would then put pictures of that kind of boat on your bathroom mirror, refrigerator, and in your work space. You would start subscribing to yachting magazines and watch online videos featuring all the newest models and their features.

These professional motivators know that the more you focus on this *thing* that you want, the more your desire for it will grow. And the more you will reorder your life and priorities to get it. Before long you are convinced that you are miserable without it and will never be happy unless you obtain it. Of course, if you do obtain it, there will be a very brief season of euphoria followed by a terrible, crushing realization. After the initial rush of excitement subsides, you're still . . . you. What's worse, this new thing suddenly presents you with a whole new list of needs and unfulfilled desires you didn't even know existed. Happiness always remains just out of reach. It's no wonder that the ultrarich battle depression and suicidal tendencies so commonly.

This dynamic is not only in effect for large items and big desires. In fact, it is even more insidious and common with more mundane things. You decide you really need a new barbecue grill. It's not in the budget, but the more you think about it, the more you feel you need it. Soon you're seemingly seeing ads for grills everywhere you look. Eventually, you break your budget by buying one. Perhaps you even use a credit card to acquire it. Now the shiny new thing is sitting on your patio and you're thinking of having friends over for a cookout. Suddenly you *hate* your old patio furniture. So before long, a new set of outdoor furniture is on the way. Which then leads to the realization that the family would really enjoy being in the backyard more if you had a pool. In fact, you *need* a pool. And on it goes.

Wise King Solomon warned us about this cycle. He wrote, "Hell and Destruction are never full; so the eyes of man are never satisfied" (Prov. 27:20). This is the lust of the eyes I mentioned previously.

This may sound harsh, but I must be very clear and direct with you here. You will never get your finances in order until you break the hold of the spirit of Mammon. That means learning to recognize the lust of the eyes when it pops up in your soul. Only then will you stop making impulse purchases and foolish spending decisions.

Only then will you break the cycle of, as the old saying goes, spending money you don't have to buy things you don't need to impress people you don't like.

A national marketing consultant, Brandon Gaille, reports that up to 20 percent of the average household's grocery bill comes from items that were purchased purely on impulse.[1] As much as twenty percent! And that's just at the grocery store! That same consultant noted,

> The old adage is that money can't buy happiness, but that's what the promise of an impulse purchase says it will provide. To some extent this is true because it feels good to grab something that is on sale. We might even talk about the amazing sale that we found and how great the deal was. The end result, however, is that there are piles of junk lying around a garage and wasted money that could have been spent on something more useful.

The ability to delay gratification—to wait for something we really want—is one of the rarest and most powerful skills in our culture. When a strong desire to buy something hits you, if you'll refuse to act on that urge and simply wait and pray, more often than not the desire will pass. It's amazing! The most intense cravings can evaporate like the dew. In the evening we can be convinced that we'll never ever be complete unless we obtain thingy xyz. Then in the cool, calm light of morning we look at that same thing and think, "Why was I so excited about that? I can take it or leave it."

> The ability to delay gratification—to wait for something we really want—is one of the rarest and most powerful skills in our culture.

This is precisely why skillful salespeople will do everything in their power to get you to act *now*. They know better than anyone that if you wait, there's a good chance you'll never buy. It is with good reason that we have the term *buyer's remorse* in our common vernacular.

By the way, having and strictly following a budget is a major tool for battling impulse buying. We'll dive into the details of the power of budgeting in an upcoming chapter. For now, it's vital that you understand the spiritual dynamic that underlies out-of-control spending. It's essential that you not fall for the oldest lie on earth—namely, that attainment of any earthly *thing* can bring you happiness.

In the Exodus account of the Israelites in the wilderness, we find God miraculously providing manna every morning. Imagine being in a barren desert yet having breakfast delivered to your door every morning! But eventually the people began to murmur and complain about this provision. They ultimately nominated a committee to go to Moses and demand some variety. "We want meat," they said. So God also miraculously provided quail. The birds flew right into the camp and offered themselves up. The Bible tells us that "while the meat was still between their teeth," the Lord grew angry with them because of their constant "craving." (Num. 11:33). Why? Because nothing on this earth can satisfy us. Only God Himself can do that.

We have a little inside joke in our house that stems back to when our kids were young teenagers. One of our sons had his sights set on some rather expensive piece of gear that he just *had* to have. He was relentless in his lobbying. This sales effort culminated with him coming to Debbie and me and declaring, "If you'll buy this for me, I promise I'll never ask you for anything else for the rest of my life."

Of course, knowing human nature, particularly teenage human nature, I knew this represented a promise he couldn't possibly keep. But sensing a teaching opportunity, I asked him if he was really serious about that vow. I thought about drawing up a written agreement and having him sign it. But instead, after Debbie and I prayed about the spending decision, we came back to him and said, "Okay, based on your promise, we're going to buy this for you. However, we're going to wait two months before we actually make the purchase." Our unspoken reasoning here was that, knowing the volatile, ever-shifting interests of the typical teen, we wanted to see if he would still be as interested then as he was at that moment. When we delivered the news, he was ecstatic and, in the rush of exhilaration, blurted out, "Awesome! I've been thinking that if we got it, we'll also need an *x*, a *y*, and probably a *z*, too!" I don't recall exactly what *x*, *y*, and *z* were, but it was additional gear that was necessary for maximizing the enjoyment of the original, rather expensive item. We instantly burst out laughing because this was the kid who had just vowed to never ask for another thing as long as he lived. Yet, before he even had this ultimate possession in his hands, he had already developed a list of new things to acquire.

I'm not singling out my son here. My point is that we're *all* this way. We all convince ourselves that the next acquisition is the one that will satisfy us. And it never is. It's a lie of the enemy.

Teach Your Children Well

It is vital that we understand that if we're going to have peace in our homes and marriages, we must fully embrace in our hearts that *things* have no power to make us happy. It is equally vital that parents understand that they are modeling the values and habits that their children will absorb and emulate.

It is a sobering thing to contemplate as a parent, but the way you view and handle money, and the place you give material possessions in your heart, will be imparted to your children. The old saying is true: It's not what you *say* that they absorb. It's what you *do*. You're modeling, with both your attitudes and your actions, how to relate to wealth and possessions.

My strong encouragement is that you never teach your family—through words or actions—that having and spending money is the answer to problems. It's not. I also exhort parents not to tell kids that they cannot have something because "we can't afford it." The message "we can't afford it" sends to kids is, "If we had more money, then we could have it." Kids internalize this as, "Money delivers happiness." Many an adult workaholic or "spen-

> Never teach your family—through words or actions—that having and spending money is the answer to problems.

daholic" started out as a child making a solemn inner vow along the lines of, "When I grow up, I'm always going to have money so I can have everything I want."

Instead, we need to be intentional about teaching our children to value what God values. And what is that? God values people. Material things decay and perish, but souls are eternal. That means love, relationships, service, loyalty, and mercy—these are the things that are truly precious in God's sight.

Teach your children the meaning behind Jesus' statement, "You cannot serve God and mammon." As we've seen, Mammon falsely promises identity, significance, independence, power, and freedom.

So, in whatever way is appropriate for their age and ability to understand, teach them that these things can *only* come from a personal relationship with God.

Everything in our popular media-driven culture—movies, music, advertising, social media—reinforces Mammon's lie that possessions provide happiness. But if you are a parent, you are the most important voice in the life of your children. That's why it is so important not to unintentionally send your children the message that the answer to every problem is more money. Jesus never offered money as an answer to a person's problem. No one ever approached Jesus with a need and heard Him say, "Do you know what you need? You need more money."

Of course, you can't impart what you don't have yourself. That's why it's so important that you allow the Spirit of God to do work in your heart and give you a proper understanding of the place and role of money.

Happily Ever After

Remember Jack and Karen from the opening of this chapter? You need to know the rest of their story. Drowning in debt and tired of all the joy, peace, and hope for the future being squeezed out of their home by financial pressure, they came into agreement with each other and with God about breaking free.

Beginning in unity, they started with one of the excellent books by my friend Dave Ramsey, which presented them with a strategy for attacking the mountain of debt that represented the primary obstacle before them. (By the way, Dave's is one of several organizations that provide great tools for helping in this area.)

Their extreme situation called for extreme austerity. While continuing to put God first through tithing, they slashed their monthly living expenses to the bone and strategically threw every spare nickel at that debt. Some people complain that trying to live on a budget squelches their creativity. I don't understand that complaint. Living on a budget forces you to become more creative. And if approached with the right attitude, it can actually be fun.

> Living on a budget forces you to become more creative. And if approached with the right attitude, it can actually be fun.

Jack and Karen stopped going out to eat and made it a kind of game to see how far they could stretch their grocery budget. They bought beans and rice in bulk and then found 101 different ways to prepare beans and rice. Instead of going to movies, they discovered countless sources of free entertainment such as free concerts in the park. Instead of subscribing to cable, they purchased a digital antenna online and got their television programming over the air for free. In doing so, they discovered something they never knew as cable subscribers—namely, that many of the local broadcast channels offered several subchannels that carried old movies and classic television series from the seventies and eighties.

In response to their demonstrated good stewardship, God blessed both of them at their jobs and their income rose dramatically. However, they didn't use the increased monthly revenue to elevate their standard of living. Instead, they kept their lifestyle the same and used the increase to accelerate their debt reduction. They found it exciting to watch the balances drop. Instead of getting fleeting gratification from indulging themselves, they learned to receive gratification from seeing that debt mountain shrink.

As a result, after just a little more than two years, they were completely debt-free. If they had done what most people do and just made the minimum payments on their debts, this young couple would have still been paying on them decades later. They traded decades of miserable servitude for two short years of self-discipline and sacrifice. But long before that last bit of debt was paid, they were already experiencing the greatest benefit of all—peace in their home and harmony in their relationship.

Today they're investing in the kingdom and in their own futures. This is the reward of wise stewardship.

You're on your way to being a wise steward, too. We're laying the groundwork in your heart and mind before we move on to the practical nuts and bolts. In the next chapter, we'll continue that process by exploring the balanced, biblical truth about debt.

CHAPTER EIGHT

THERE IS ENOUGH

Charles Ponzi. He's the infamous individual whose name is now forever associated with a particular type of financial scam...the Ponzi scheme.

In the early 1920s, the smooth-talking con man living in Boston founded an official-sounding investment firm called the Securities Exchange Company. His pitch to prospective investors was straightforward. Invest $100 with him and he'd deliver an astonishing 50 percent return on the investment within forty-five days. Keep it with him for a full ninety days and he'd deliver a full 100 percent return! This, in a day in which traditional savings accounts were paying about 3 percent.

These kinds of results sounded too good to be true, and indeed they were. Yet this was the beginning of the Roaring Twenties, and at the time it seemed like everyone knew someone who was getting rich in the booming stock market. As a result, Ponzi found eighteen people who bought his sales pitch and forked over $100—a sizable sum in that day. At the end of forty-five days, Ponzi took some of the money he'd recently collected from new investors and used it to provide the original investors the amazing 50 percent returns he'd promised. Of course, most didn't want out. They wanted to keep their money with Ponzi so it would earn even more. With dollar signs in their eyes and what seemed like a bona fide get-rich-quick opportunity before them, they poured even more savings into Ponzi's hands.

They also told all their friends and relatives about the amazing investment deal they'd discovered. Of course, all these wanted in, too. As a result, a rapidly growing stream of new investors flowed into Ponzi's fund. And in each case, Ponzi delivered on his outrageous promise—not with genuine returns on an investment but by simply using the money of newer investors to pay the earlier ones who cashed out. Fortunately for Ponzi, once greed took hold, very few wanted to cash out. Within six months of launching his endeavor, investors had placed nearly $2.5 million in Ponzi's hands (roughly $30 million in today's dollars). After another month he was hauling in an additional $1 million per week. Another month after that, it had surged to $1 million per *day*.

Ponzi could only keep this merry-go-round going as long as far more people poured into the fund than wanted out. But eventually, a few skeptical newspaper articles were published, and the stream of new investors dried up. As a result, the whole scam collapsed with breathtaking speed. Ponzi went to prison while the majority of the investors never saw a dime of their money. Many of these were working-class Bostonians who'd invested their life savings. For example, it was estimated that 75 percent of Boston's police force had invested in the fraudulent scheme.[1]

Ponzi's scam has been repeated many times and in various forms in the nearly one hundred years since then. It always ends badly, with the investors who come in toward the end invariably left out in the cold with nothing but an expensive, painful lesson to show for it.

The Most Common Scam of All

I'm sure you would agree that anyone who runs a Ponzi scheme is despicable. A person who would deceptively defraud another gullible person is obviously not a good human being. Well, as I write these words, millions of people are running what amounts to a Ponzi scheme on themselves. That's right. On *themselves*. Much like Charles Ponzi did to others, they have conned themselves into believing something ridiculous. In a similar way, keeping the scam going will require getting ever-larger sums of money in the future to pay for the promises of the past. And like Mr. Ponzi's operation, it can only end in heartache and tears.

> Millions of people are running what amounts to a Ponzi scheme on themselves.

I'm talking about people who count on future earnings to pay present expenditures. This is precisely what a person does when using credit or financing to buy something they can't actually afford. When you do that, you're committing money you haven't received yet to buy something you want now. And just like any other scam, it actually constitutes stealing. I'll explain why in a moment.

First, allow me to revisit a subject I briefly touched on in the previous chapter. We all like to think that we are rational, thoughtful, logical people. When challenged, we can come up with an ironclad defense for every decision we make and every action we take. But the reality is, most of our decisions are rooted in emotion, rather than logic. That is certainly true where spending decisions are concerned. Here is how that works. Our internal "wanter" gets to wanting something—usually because we've fallen for Mammon's tired lie that obtaining that thing, whatever it is, will make us happier or more significant. This all takes place at an emotional level. Usually these emotions stem from trying to numb some sort of pain, quell a fear, shore up insecurity, or feed pride. Once the emotion is present, all that is necessary to take action is to get the brain to sign off on the decision. This is where our amazing ability to rationalize what we want comes in.

Once the gut-level emotion driving the decision is stirred up—fear, insecurity, pride, envy, lust, etc.—only then do we start building a case for it with logic. This explains why the most common reason given for impulse buying is that the item was "on sale." In fact, one study revealed that 88 percent of all impulse purchases were explained this way.[2] A sale price gives your head a ready-made rationale for doing what your gut has already decided it wants. I have a friend who used to make a lot of impulse purchases using the "it was on sale" defense. "Look at how much we saved!" he'd say. Ultimately, his more frugal wife had to tell him, "Honey, we can't afford for you to save us any more money this month. All this 'saving' is going to bankrupt us."

An article on the CBS Moneywatch website cited a poll in which 54 percent of the respondents admitted to recently spending $100 or more on an impulse buy. A full 20 percent said they'd spent at least $1,000 on an impulse purchase.[3] The same research also reveals that most people admit that buying something puts them in a better mood (at least momentarily). This isn't surprising when you understand the neuroscience and brain chemistry behind it. For many people, buying something they crave creates a release of "feel good" brain chemicals called endorphins. The acquisition of something shiny and new delivers a momentary "rush" that is addictive. Being a "shopaholic" isn't a cute euphemism. Addiction to buying is a very real thing. Yes, God created those reward systems in the brain to help us experience love in relationships and to feel a thrill at achieving a goal. But the enemy tries to turn those God-given systems against us.

It's been more than twenty-five years, but I still recall encountering a couple, Pam and Eric, on the verge of divorce because she had developed a shopping addiction that she'd somehow managed to keep hidden from her husband for several years. Eric was a driven workaholic who delegated all the details of the household finances to Pam. He was focused solely on winning in his sales career and climbing the ladder at work. This left Pam largely on her own and wholly unaccountable for how she spent their fairly sizable income. Feeling unloved and bored, she eventually started filling the voids in her life by shopping. The thrill of the purchase briefly enhanced her mood.

Even though Eric earned a great income, she eventually found herself hitting the limits on their credit cards. Instead of throttling back on her spending, she applied for new cards without Eric knowing about it. She would transfer the balances on her old cards to the new ones. Of course, these cards were eventually maxed out as well. Soon the minimum payments on these cards were more than she could cover with the family's cash flow. Her solution was to acquire additional credit cards and take cash advances to pay the minimum payments on others.

This unfolded over the course of a couple of years. Not surprisingly, the stress of juggling all of this combined with the fear of being found out began to take a terrible toll on Pam's mental and physical health. As you might expect, the whole fragile house of cards eventually collapsed. Eric, who blissfully considered himself a financial success because of his income, discovered the truth in a car dealership one day when trying to buy a new luxury vehicle. The dealership pulled his credit report and the stunning truth of his actual financial situation landed on him like a house.

Naturally, he felt betrayed and angry. But in reality the situation was, at least in part, a result of his complete abdication of his role in the marriage partnership. What Pam did was wrong and foolish. But it was driven largely by a gaping hole in her heart that God designed love and affection to fill.

Without a doubt, spending money can be a powerful drug. It may be the most powerful drug of all. And like most highs, the addict needs ever bigger or more frequent doses to get the same effect.

Keep in mind, Eric and Pam's financial train wreck occurred decades ago—before the internet, Amazon, iPhones, and one-click buying made it easier than ever to feed that kind of addiction. Is it any wonder that the typical American today has less financial margin than ever before? In a 2016 study, nearly two-thirds of those surveyed reported they wouldn't be able to handle an unexpected $500 car repair or a $1,000 emergency room bill.[4] Many people are utterly unprepared for an unanticipated expense because their spending is out of control.

Piling up debt today that you presume you'll be able to pay with money you expect to earn in the future is essentially running a Ponzi scam on yourself.

Thou Shalt Not Steal from Thy Future Self

This likely won't come as a shock to you, but God is against stealing. It's true. He put Himself clearly on the record on this issue

> What many
> Christians don't
> realize is that
> spending money
> you don't have is a
> form of stealing.

way back in Exodus when he delivered the Ten Commandments to the
Israelites (see Exod. 20:15). What
many Christians don't realize is that
spending money you don't have is a
form of stealing. It's stealing from
your future. And from your family's future. You're reaching into the
future and robbing yourself of choices. Robbing yourself of freedom. Of peace.

This kind of theft is a symptom of a deeper issue—our inability
to wait. We want what we want—now. I recently read that a significant and growing percentage of Americans who have a tax refund
coming to them actually have spent the money before they get the
refund.[5] Because they know it's coming, they run out and make
a purchase, probably on credit, before the money is even in their
hands. Once the money does arrive, I suspect some don't use it to
pay the loan or credit card balance but instead spend it on something else. In other words, they spend the money twice.

This is tragically wrong. It's theft...from yourself. More significantly, it's theft from the impact God planned for you to have for
His kingdom. It's a vicious cycle and the only way to break it is to
cut yourself off cold turkey. To completely stop spending money
you don't have. Of course, that requires learning to wait. It means if
you really want something, save for it.

Allow me to tell you why this is the spiritual way to approach buying things. The insight I want to show you is hidden in a Bible verse that contains the word *hope* no fewer than four times. Here it is:

For in hope we have been saved, but hope that is seen is not hope; for who hopes for what he already sees? (Romans 8:24 NASB)

Here Paul asks, "Why does one still hope for what he already sees?" Let me paraphrase Paul's question: Why would someone keep hoping for something he already has? Once you have something, you stop hoping for it.

Here's the important message embedded in this verse. God wired you to operate on hope. Hope is more than just wishing. It is a powerful spiritual force that God uniquely created us to contain in our hearts. He created it to serve as fuel for perseverance. Hope empowers you to delay gratification so you can experience true, deep joy and satisfaction when the thing for which you've hoped finally becomes a reality.

Need a biblical example? Abraham desperately wanted a son and, at a key moment in his life, had an encounter with God in which God promised him one. Soon, however, Abraham grew weary of waiting and tried to make something happen in his own power. He looked for and found a shortcut. Like people who borrow from the future to obtain what they desire in the present, the birth of Ishmael created nothing but problems and heartache. Then Abraham went back to waiting on God and ultimately, through faith, saw God's promise fulfilled. What fueled Abraham's faith-filled waiting? Paul tells us:

Even when there was no reason for hope, Abraham kept hoping—believing that he would become the father of many nations. (Romans 4:18 NLT)

Hope! God wired you so that if you wanted something that is good and from Him, you would be filled with hope. And that hope would be a force moving you forward in faith-filled anticipation and patient perseverance. God cares about the process. There is gold in the process. There is growth in the process. And hope keeps the fire of faith burning throughout the process God has ordained for you, for your own benefit and blessing. Then, when the day of fulfillment arrives, you experience a quality of joy and satisfaction that is both meaningful and long lasting.

> There is gold in the process. There is growth in the process.

This explains why debt is so insidious. Borrowing kills hope! Throwing down a credit card when you want something destroys the process. Remember what Paul said? "Who hopes for what he already sees?" Instant gratification—stealing from your own future—provides a momentary rush of excitement that quickly fades and becomes corrosive. This is exactly what Proverbs 20:17 is referring to when it says, "Stolen bread tastes sweet, but it turns to gravel in the mouth" (NLT).

Please hear me. The buy-now-and-pay-later lifestyle is financial suicide—both individually and as a culture. Personal indebtedness among Americans is soaring.[6] We also have one of the highest rates of depression in the developed world.[7] These two statistics are related. Why? Because we're violating a key principle concerning the way God created us. We're designed to run on hope, and borrowing is a hope killer. Of course, as we've already seen, debt brings misery and depression in other ways. And our generation is drowning in it.

Do you realize that my fellow baby boomers and I are the first American generation to do this? The levels of debt in which we've buried ourselves are unprecedented in history. Of course, debt has been around as long as there have been people. There is a reason why God, through Moses, gave His people specific *usury* laws concerning loaning money at interest back around 1500 BC. But archaeologists in Iraq have unearthed clay tablets that record loans and interest terms dating back as far as 3500 BC!

Yes, historically other societies have gone into debt bondage, but not like this generation. My parents didn't live this way. My grandparents didn't live this way. They saved, waited, and bought with cash.

Now, it may surprise you to learn that many of the debt instruments so readily available today are relatively recent inventions. For example, mortgages as we currently understand them weren't widely available or in use until the mid-1930s—the height of the Great Depression. I find it interesting that the Great Recession of 2007–2009, also known as the "global liquidity crisis," was largely triggered by a wave of defaults in the repayment of "subprime" mortgage loans. In other words, millions of people were loaned money to buy houses—often with little to no money down—for amounts they had no business borrowing and that they couldn't possibly ever repay. Everyone in the system was simply betting on home values climbing rapidly forever. As we now know, they didn't keep rising. They couldn't.

In contrast, with those first mortgage loans back in the 1930s you couldn't borrow more than 50 percent of the property's market value. In other words, borrowers had to have a 50 percent down payment. Today the typical loan length is thirty years, but back then the repayment schedule was spread over three to five years and ended with a balloon payment. In other words, if you borrowed money to buy a house, you ended up owning it free and clear in no more than five years.

Today you can finance a car for eight years. A car! Anyone foolish enough to do this will be "upside down" on the vehicle for most, if not all, of its useful life.

The credit card was essentially invented by American Airlines in the 1930s. At the time, air travel was so expensive only the wealthy could afford to fly. American came up with the idea of a card that would allow middle-class folks to purchase a ticket with the card, and then pay it out in a few installments (fly now, pay later). Other airlines quickly followed suit.

In the 1950s, the success of this approach, aided by the first breakthroughs in computerized record keeping using giant mainframe computers, led to the creation of the Diners Club card, and then a little later, the American Express card. Keep in mind that these were "charge cards," not "credit cards," meaning that the balance charged was due in full each month. You could not carry a balance on these cards and therefore no interest charges were applied. Around 1960, one of the first true credit cards emerged in the form of the BankAmericard, now called Visa. This was a true credit card, which enabled consumers to carry a balance and, of course, incur hefty interest charges. The Western world has never been the same.

Our grandparents didn't have the myriad of easy ways to get buried in debt. But more importantly, their values wouldn't allow it. They believed in paying as you go, rather than buying now, paying later. Obviously, they didn't buy on credit cards because they didn't exist. Yet, they are so ubiquitous now that even kids are getting credit card applications. When my children were still at home, I was shocked to see them receiving credit card applications in the mail consistently. I remember opening one particular credit card application addressed to my fifteen-year-old son. They were offering him a larger credit line than they were willing to give me. He didn't even have a job, but they were going to allow him to bury himself in credit card debt before he could even drive.

Today young people are graduating from college with more debt and a much higher debt ratio than our parents had after thirty or forty years of living. As I write, Americans owe nearly $1.5 trillion (yes, that's trillion with a *t*) in student loan debt. That mountain of debt is being carried by roughly 44 million borrowers.[8] To put that in perspective, that's about $620 billion more than the already staggeringly high total of US credit card debt.

College graduates in the class of 2017 entered the world of work carrying, on average, $39,400 in student loan debt.[9] That's just the average. Many who pursued graduate degrees from elite private universities are emerging with more than $100,000 of debt—often with liberal arts degrees that have limited utility in the job market. A significant percentage of the most deeply indebted of these graduates can only find jobs in the service sector—waiting tables, tending bar, and brewing coffee. Those jobs represent good, honest work. But they don't require an expensive college degree.

Not surprisingly, the current student loan delinquency rate— defined as ninety or more days behind in loan payments—is 11.2 percent and rising.[10] But under current law, not even bankruptcy can erase these debts. Barring either a miracle or years of sound, biblical stewardship, many will be dragging these loans around for the rest of their lives—crippling their ability to buy a home or, for many, even move out of their parents' homes. In 2014, nearly a third of all young adults age eighteen to thirty-four were living with their parents.[11] A third!

The fact is that our whole society is drowning in a sea of debt. Is it any wonder that, as a culture, we are becoming the most depressed people on earth? We killed our hope. We stole from our futures to pay for present expenses in history's largest group Ponzi scheme.

If you're in this situation, you're obviously not alone. Untold millions are right there with you. But there is encouragement in Abraham's story. Please note that he killed hope and went for quick gratification by fathering Ishmael. He was in a real mess. But then he took the painful steps necessary to restart, reset, and move back into hope. Ultimately, he saw his heart's desire realized in a way that was consistent with God's good plan and timing. His miracle son, Isaac, was an enormous blessing not only to Abraham and Sarah but also to the whole world because he represented the formation of the lineage of Jesus.

> Abraham took the painful steps necessary to restart, reset, and move back into hope.

Please note the words of wise King Solomon in Proverbs 13:12: "Hope deferred makes the heart sick, but when the desire comes, it is a tree of life." Many people today are heartsick because they've killed their hope. But if we learn to wait in hope, we'll find that obtaining things God's way and in God's timing is indeed a "tree of life"—producing the fruit of joy and satisfaction that is as long-lived and stable as a tree.

Proverbs 10:22 says, "The blessing of the LORD makes one rich, and He adds no sorrow with it." Allow me to paraphrase that message: When you are increased through God's blessing (rather than trying to bless yourself), there is no sorrow mixed in with that increase. The converse is also true. When you refuse to wait on God in hope, any increase you obtain will come mixed with grief and sadness.

Makers vs. Takers

I don't mean to sound like a prophet of doom for American society. I simply aim to provide the biblical diagnosis of our financial illness so the Bible can prescribe the appropriate spiritual remedy. As we've already seen, a key symptom of this disease is our inability to wait for anything. This in turn produces an epidemic of bondage to debt and joylessness in living.

Another troubling symptom is the twofold trend in our culture toward tearing down the productive and diligent as exploiters while simultaneously elevating the unproductive and lackadaisical as victims. You might call this trend the enterprising versus the entitled. Put another way, it's makers versus takers.

The fact is that one of the primary reasons our nation stands wobbling on the edge of an economic abyss is that too many people in our culture are taking more than they are making. Having been raised under the affirming mantras of "Follow your dreams" and "You're special," several generations have come to believe life, the world, and society owe them a good life. And when they don't get it, they get angry and bitter.

What defines a maker as opposed to a taker? Makers work hard. They consistently deliver more value than they're getting paid for. They save and invest. And many start and grow businesses that create jobs.

Entrepreneurs and business owners should be hailed as heroes in our nation. Sadly, they are some of the most reviled and detested people in the eyes of the popular culture. Starting a business is one of the most difficult and labor-intensive things a person can do. Success requires extreme work hours, high levels of risk, and, in our currently hostile business environment, navigating a bewildering obstacle course of regulations, taxes, and paperwork requirements. Yet movies and television programs routinely portray business owners as mean, greedy, exploitative, and dishonest people who lie around and profit from the sweat of others. It's a rare drama that doesn't make the villain either a successful business owner or the head of a corporation. Indeed, the more successful a person is in business, the more likely they are to be viewed with suspicion these days. Yet these are precisely the people who provide good jobs and opportunities. We can't all work for the government. Roughly half of all the jobs in our economy are created and maintained in small-to medium-sized businesses.

Businesses create wealth. The gross domestic product (GDP) of the United States in 1917 was $59.7 billion (in inflation-adjusted terms). In 2017 it was $19.3 trillion. That's more than a three hundred–fold increase in one hundred years. This growth didn't occur because wealth was transferred from other nations. It was created. Enterprising people found ways to turn sweat and ingenuity into something tangible and valuable.

> Enterprising people found ways to turn sweat and ingenuity into something tangible and valuable.

Growing a successful business is not stealing! This is not to say there aren't some dishonest business people or unscrupulous companies. But starting a business is an act of courage. And growing one requires extraordinary effort.

On the "takers" end of the spectrum are those who accept a job and then deliver the bare minimum effort to get by. They happily take a regular paycheck while they cut corners and slide by wherever possible. Sadly, many Christians are guilty of this. Yet this is a form of stealing, and it is something God simply cannot and will not bless.

Trust Is the Key

As we've seen, some Christian people steal. They may steal from others. Or, more commonly, they steal from their own futures. The question is why. I believe there is only one reason some Christians steal. It can only be because they don't trust God to provide for them. God has promised to provide for our needs and declared plainly that we'll find real happiness only in our relationship with Him. We would only steal—from others or from ourselves—if we don't believe Him. We don't believe He is good, faithful, and trustworthy. We don't really believe He will provide. We don't believe there is enough for us. We don't trust Him to bless us, so we take it into our hands to bless ourselves.

The bottom line is don't be a slave to immediate gratification. Don't steal from your own future. Learn to wait and you'll experience real joy. Learn to save and you will have more than enough. In the next chapter I'll share a powerful attribute that will help you do all that and more.

CHAPTER NINE

GREAT GAIN

A hundred years before anyone was concerned about keeping up with the Kardashians, people were "keeping up with the Joneses." I'm sure you've heard that phrase all your life, but you may not know where it originated.

Keeping Up with the Joneses was a cartoon strip that appeared in the "funny papers" across the nation from 1913 to 1939. The creator, Pop Momand, crafted the McGinnis family to poke fun at a growing societal trend in America—the powerful need to focus our lives and spending on impressing other people. The cartoon family—comprised of a husband and wife and their teenage daughter—was obsessed with their wealthier, more fashionable neighbors, the Jones family. Readers never actually saw the Joneses. But they constantly heard about them through reports from Mrs. McGinnis and their daughter. If the Joneses bought something, the McGinnises had to have it, too. The humor of the comic strip was rooted in watching a family constantly twisting themselves into knots to buy things, not because they wanted them, needed them, or cared about them, but solely in a desperate effort to appear to be something they really weren't. It was a comical personification of that tendency I mentioned in chapter 7—namely, to spend money we don't have to buy things we don't need to impress people we don't like.

The appearance of that particular comic strip at the beginning of the twentieth century is no coincidence. It was right around then that a new innovation in communication was entering homes and impacting the minds of Americans on a massive scale (sound familiar?). No, I'm not talking about the telephone. I'm referring to the consumer magazine.

Prior to the turn of the last century, magazines were costly to print and very expensive to mail. As a result, the few magazines that existed were targeted at the rich in a handful of major cities. Two developments changed that. The first was the invention in the late 1800s of new high-volume printing presses. The other was the introduction by the US Postal Service of the "second-class mail" category for publications. Suddenly, it became economically feasible to create magazines targeted at the middle and working classes and not only deliver them in bulk to newsstands in big cities, but also mail them directly into homes across small-town America. Subscription rates plunged to around ten cents an issue because the magazines made their profits by selling advertising.

Some of the most popular of these among women were magazines focusing on fashion, home décor, homemaking, and celebrity lifestyles. Men's magazines focusing on cars, sports, and outdoor activities flourished as well. Of course, this era coincided with an explosion of new technologies and inventions that brought a dizzying array of new consumer goods to the market. And the advertisers of these new convenience items and luxury goods correctly saw these magazines as the ideal vehicle for targeting their messages to the right groups.

Advertising rapidly evolved into both an art and a science, aimed at getting people to feel dissatisfied with their lives as they currently existed. To the advertiser, *contentment* was the enemy. Advertisers knew that in order to succeed, contentment had to be eroded. And they have only gotten better at it in the last hundred years.

The Power of Contentment

Yes, if you're trying to get large numbers of people to part with their hard-earned money to buy your new widget, you have to find a way to make them feel discontented, at least with the facet of their lives that your widget affects. That's why, in our entrepreneurial, consumer-driven society, your sense of contentment is under constant media assault from every side.

Contentment is a powerful thing. Who says? Paul does. In the Word of God. First Timothy 6:6 says, "Now godliness with contentment is great gain." The gain Paul is referring to here isn't necessarily material gain, although the contented believer is indeed much more "blessable" than the discontented one, as we're about to see. But Paul is talking about far more than money here. When you combine

> When you combine "godliness"—that is, putting God first in your priorities—with contentment, you gain peace.

"godliness"—that is, putting God first in your priorities—with contentment, you gain peace. You gain confidence. You gain security. Above all, you gain freedom. You see, discontentment makes you a prisoner to your own cravings, trapping you in a never-ending cycle of acquisition and disappointment.

Do you remember Andy's testimony at the beginning of chapter 6? He was the gentleman who, on a humanitarian trip to Angola, discovered that he had allowed a focus on what others had to destroy his sense of gratitude for all the good things the Lord had given him. Andy's problem had a root cause. It began with the same mistake countless other believers make—especially in our day. That mistake is inviting contentment's worst enemy into your heart.

The Enemy of Contentment

Yes, contentment has an enemy. It goes by the name *comparison*. Few things will dissolve your sense of contentment and gratitude faster than the habit of comparing your life and situation to those of others. It's a slippery slope that results in us sliding rapidly down into a swamp of resentment, envy, discouragement, and pride. God does not want us comparing ourselves to others. In fact, it's a sin.

I've observed that women tend to notice each other's purses and shoes. Men notice each other's watches and cars. Both sexes use these cues to gauge their status and prosperity relative to others'. But it's a dangerous game.

Once you're living in comparison mode, you are constantly evaluating and scoring every person, every circumstance, and every possession you encounter in relation to .yourself, your circumstances, and your possessions. And that evaluation can essentially be boiled down to a simple binary judgment of "better than" or "worse than." Every encounter, every waking minute of every day becomes an exercise in determining, "Am I doing better or worse than this person? Is my house better or worse? Is my spouse better or worse?" And depending on how you answer the question each time, you're either feeding insecurity or pride. You're feeding either a sense of inferiority or one of superiority through comparison. Neither are of God. Indeed, both are rooted in the spirit of Mammon.

Comparison is also a sin because it invariably produces anger and resentment toward God. Once you're focused on your neighbor who seems to be doing better, it's not a long step over into blaming your heavenly Father and questioning His goodness and care. Please notice that I said a neighbor who "seems" to be doing better. The truth is you don't know what's going on behind the closed doors of his or her home, much less what's going on in the confines of his or her soul. You don't know what darkness, hurts, grief, or despair a person may be concealing behind a smiling facade. Yet when we compare our outward circumstance to theirs, we're in grave danger of developing an angry, ungrateful heart toward our sweet, gracious Father.

> When we compare our outward circumstance to others, we're in danger of developing an angry, ungrateful heart toward our sweet, gracious Father.

Comparison opens the door to one of the ugliest sins of all—envy. How ugly? Well, the Bible tells us that it was envy that motivated the religious leaders in Jesus' day to have Him crucified:

> But Pilate answered them, saying, "Do you want me to release to you the King of the Jews?" For he knew that the chief priests had handed Him over *because of envy*. (Mark 15:9–10, emphasis added)

That's right—when Satan wanted to inspire a group of people to brutally kill the sinless Son of God, his weapon of choice was envy. It's that powerful. It's that dark. That's why it is so vital to avoid the comparison trap.

When you focus on someone else's situation, you take your focus off God's good plan for your life. In Hebrews 12:1, the Word of God exhorts us all to "run with endurance the race that is set before us." God has set a race before you that only you can run. Your race is unique to the one-of-a-kind set of gifts and callings God has placed upon you, and to the specific role He created you to play in His kingdom plans and purposes. Run *your* race. That means keeping your eyes on the Lord and *your* path—and off whatever is required for the races of others. Following Jesus' resurrection and before His ascension into heaven, Peter and Jesus were having a conversation about Peter's future and fate. In the middle of that talk, Peter pointed to John, following at a distance:

Peter, seeing him, said to Jesus, "But Lord, what about this man?" Jesus said to him, "If I will that he remain till I come, what is that to you? You follow Me." (John 21:21–22)

Allow me to paraphrase Jesus' response to Peter: "Run your race. And let John run his." We will only be truly happy when we're in the center of God's will doing what He created us to do. You see, real joy comes from purpose, not pleasure. Here's what I mean by that.

Deep genuine happiness and fulfillment stem from living out your true purpose, not experiencing worldly, carnal pleasure. If you're fulfilling the purpose for which God created you, you can have nothing and still be deliriously happy and content. Conversely,

> You can have everything the world says you should desire, and if you're not living out your God-given purpose, you'll be utterly miserable.

you can have everything the world says you should desire, and if you're not living out your God-given purpose, you'll be utterly miserable. If you lose your direction, you will lose your happiness. This is why the comparison trap is such a serious pitfall.

Yes, contentment has an enemy. But it also has an opposite.

The Opposite of Contentment

There is an antique, King James–y word that we don't use much anymore, but it describes a sin that really is the very opposite of contentment. *Covetousness.*

It describes the practice of craving what someone else possesses. This deadly habit is the focus of the tenth commandment God gave Moses.

> You shall not covet your neighbor's house; you shall not covet your neighbor's wife, nor his male servant, nor his female servant, nor his ox, nor his donkey, nor anything that is your neighbor's. (Exodus 20:17)

In today's vernacular, God might instead say, "You shall not try to keep up with the Joneses." Clearly, God does not want us comparing ourselves with others financially. Let me tell you what you're doing when you feel resentment, sadness, or disappointment when someone you know gets a new house, a nicer car, or takes an exotic vacation. You're opening the door to covetousness, and when you covet, you're in very dangerous territory. When you open the door to covetousness, you open a hellish portal that all kinds of evil can come pouring through.

Jesus Himself sternly warned His disciples about this danger:

And He said to them, "Take heed and beware of covetousness, for one's life does not consist in the abundance of the things he possesses." (Luke 12:15)

The New Living Translation of that verse reads, "Beware! Guard against every kind of greed. Life is not measured by how much you own." That would be a great verse to memorize. *Life is not measured by how much you own!*

According to Colossians 3:5, coveting is actually a form of idolatry. That's right—idol worship! How can this be? You'll recall that idolatry is essentially looking to something other than God for your sense of significance and fulfillment. When you allow covetousness to destroy your sense of contentment, you make whatever it is you're coveting a false god. It's actually even worse. You've given the person whose goods or situation you covet a power over you that only God should have. The Holy Spirit should determine when and how you spend your money. But when you're committed to keeping up with the Joneses, you surrender to the Joneses that decision-making power. If Mr. Jones gets a new SUV, covetousness forces you to get a new SUV. If Mrs. Jones buys a new designer purse, you're forced to either run out and buy one or be miserable.

Your "lord" is whoever you allow to set your priorities. And coveting gives another person the power to set your priorities rather than Jesus, who is the true, rightful Lord of your life.

If you're still unsure about the truth that covetousness is the opposite of contentment, allow me to share another verse with you:

> Let your conduct be without covetousness; be content with such things as you have. For He Himself has said, "I will never leave you nor forsake you." (Hebrews 13:5)

First, notice that covetousness and contentment are contrasted there in the first part of that verse. Being content is presented as the alternative to coveting. That's because they are opposites. They are mutually exclusive, meaning that you can't be both at the same time. If you're coveting, you're not content. However, I find it interesting that the only part of that verse most people ever quote is the second half. I understand why. It's a wonderful promise. There the writer of Hebrews gives us the reason we should be content rather than covetous. "For He Himself has said, 'I will never leave you nor forsake you.'" I've heard those words quoted thousands of times. I've quoted them myself more times than I can count. "I will never leave you nor forsake you" is a wonderful promise of God. But what we've missed is that this promise wasn't given out of the blue. It was given as a reason for being content with what we have.

Here's what God is saying: "Why would you ever covet what someone else has when you have Me?" Or put another way, "Why would you ever feel insecure or insignificant or unfulfilled when the God of the universe loves you and wants to be in intimate relationship with you?"

It's a great question. Why would you covet if aware of that truth? Why would you not be content after God Himself has looked you in the eyes and with covenantal love said, "I'm not going anywhere. I'll never leave you. And I'll never let you down"? In that light, craving what someone else possesses seems so absurd. And yet countless believers do that very thing.

I vividly recall a day a few years ago in which I was thinking about this very verse of Scripture in my quiet time. As I pondered the words "I will never leave you nor forsake you," I was reminded of what Jesus cried out on the cross: "My God, My God, why have You forsaken Me?" (Matt. 27:46). Of course, I was well aware that Jesus was actually quoting from the twenty-second psalm when He said those words. I've read and even preached about those words from the cross many times. But in that particular moment I saw them in a new light.

I suddenly realized that Jesus wasn't just quoting a Messianic Scripture. That particular psalm and Scripture came to His mind because that's what He was experiencing in that moment. In other words, God actually forsook Jesus as He was hanging on the cross bearing the sin, guilt, and shame of all humankind. Of course, Jesus can't lie. So if we hear Him asking God why God has forsaken Him, it could only be because that is precisely what has happened. The Greek word translated as "forsake" in that verse (*egkataleipo*) means to "leave in straits, leave helpless, totally abandoned, utterly forsaken."[1]

As I contemplated that reality in my quiet time that day, I asked God the same question Jesus asked. I said, "Father, why did you forsake Jesus?" In my spirit, I instantly heard the familiar voice of God give this reply:

"So I would never forsake you."

In the same way Jesus bore our sin so we could receive His righteousness, Jesus bore our rejection so we could receive God's acceptance.

> The very reason God could make the promise "I will never leave you nor forsake you" is Jesus bore that for you and me.

The very reason God could make the promise "I will never leave you nor forsake you" is Jesus bore that for you and me.

This is why we can be content rather than covetous. It's why we can live in gratitude and generosity rather than in resentment and striving. The peace and security of having Him—His love, His fellowship, His presence—frees us from the never-ending cycle of comparison and coveting and craving.

If you've been a poor steward up until this point in your life, it doesn't change the reality of God's love and faithfulness. He still says, "I will never leave you nor forsake you." If you've really made a mess of your finances, I want you to understand something: God is not going to leave you. You may even walk away from God for a season, but He will never leave you. You can know that because He abandoned His own Son, instead. Just so you could be secure in His love and care.

Are you beginning to comprehend how completely inappropriate it is for a child of God to live in envy and jealousy toward any other person?

The Key to Contentment

The vital foundation of a life of contentment is simply understanding that no possession, no achievement, no position, and no person on this earth can fulfill the deepest longings of your heart. Only God can do that. No new job, no promotion, no house or car or recognition can satisfy you.

Material things are temporary, fleeting, prone to rust, decay, and deterioration. In contrast, the things of God are eternal. One hundred thousand years after that car you've just *got* to have has turned to rusty powder, the souls you've impacted for the kingdom of God will still be around.

Please don't misunderstand. This isn't to say that God is against you having and enjoying things. God loves to bless His children and see them satisfied, not just in the life to come but in this life. As the psalmist wrote,

Bless the LORD, O my soul,
and forget not all His benefits:
who forgives all your iniquities,
who heals all your diseases,
who redeems your life from destruction,
who crowns you with lovingkindness and tender mercies,
who satisfies your mouth with good things,
so that your youth is renewed like the eagle's. (Psalm 103:2–5)

The Lord loves to satisfy His children with good things. But He is only fully free to do so when He knows our hearts won't go after those things. That our delight will continue to be in Him. That we won't turn what He intends to be blessings into idols.

What's more, God created us to be achievers, creators, expanders, cultivators, restorers, and growers. When He put Adam and Eve in the garden, He gave them a mandate to cultivate and keep the garden. He also commanded them to be fruitful, multiply, fill the earth, and take dominion over it. In other words, our desire for growth, increase, and development is from Him. It's something He put within us to carry out the mission He gave

> God created us to be achievers, creators, expanders, cultivators, restorers, and growers.

us. As we've seen, good stewards grow what God has placed in their hands.

The key here is understanding the difference between aspiring to *become* something or to *build* something, as opposed to simply lusting to *have* something. Far too many people go into business not because they're passionate about what they're doing, but simply because they view it as an avenue for obtaining wealth. Invariably, get-rich-fast businesses lead only to dissatisfaction.

I know a very smart, highly driven man who, right out of college, made it his life goal to attain a certain level of wealth by the age of forty. That was his clear, stated objective—to have a certain net worth in dollars by the time he turned forty. He chose the oil and gas business precisely because it offered the possibility of achieving that kind of wealth.

He worked relentlessly, with a tremendous, almost obsessive focus to become successful. And he did. In fact, when he reached his fortieth birthday, he had indeed attained his goal. He could retire and never have to think about money for the rest of his life. He was enormously "successful" and had obtained much of what this world tells us will provide happiness and contentment.

That man told me that the year following that milestone birthday was by far the worst year of his life. He said he was completely miserable and fell into what a psychiatrist diagnosed as clinical depression. It was a year of complete despair and despondency. Now, this man had grown up in a Christian home and had given his life to Christ as a child but as an adult had not had much time for God while chasing his all-consuming goal. What Jesus said was true. A man cannot serve two masters. You can't worship God if you're worshipping Mammon.

Toward the end of that year of complete darkness and misery, this man turned to God in desperation. "I finally cried out to the Lord," he told me. "I prayed, 'Lord, what is it? What's wrong with me?'" He told me that God's gentle reply was simply, "Son, money doesn't satisfy. I'm the only one who can satisfy your soul."

As he finished his testimony, I'll never forget what this gentleman said next. "Robert, do you want to know what the first forty years of my life taught me? I learned that if your goal is to climb to the top, there is only one thing left to do when you reach your goal. Jump off. There is nowhere else to climb."

Dear reader, do you know you can never climb to the top of God? When you make your primary goal a relationship with Him, you'll never reach the end of all the wonderful things there are to discover. His wonders and glory and goodness are inexhaustible. Every time you think you must have discovered all of Him, you turn a corner and find a whole new unexplored realm of His love. And He is the only one who can satisfy. As we saw in Psalm 103:5, He is the one who "satisfies your mouth with good things." In another psalm, David reminds us,

The LORD upholds all who fall,
and raises up all who are bowed down.
The eyes of all look expectantly to You,
and You give them their food in due season.
You open Your hand
and satisfy the desire of every living thing. (Psalm 145:14–16,
    emphasis added)

This is the God we serve. When we have Him, we have the only One who can truly satisfy us at the level of spirit and soul. Plus, everything we need in life comes with Him. When we put Him first, we don't have to be concerned with material things. Remember, when we seek first the kingdom, all those other things like food, clothing, and housing are added to us (Matt. 6:33). Your heavenly Father knows what you need and delights in providing it. All you have to do is keep your worship where it belongs—on Him.

Given all that, why would you concern yourself with keeping up with the Joneses when the Joneses are probably miserable and depressed and making no eternal impact for the kingdom of God?

Why would you ever allow yourself to fall into the trap of comparing yourself with others? Comparison is the enemy of contentment. Run *your* race. It's unlike that of anyone else who has ever lived! Why would you covet what your neighbor has when you're not called to run his race and when stuff carries no ability to satisfy you? Why would you not be content when the God of heaven and earth has looked at you with love in His eyes and promised, "I will never leave you nor forsake you"?

> Run *your* race. It's unlike that of anyone else who has ever lived!

God says:

"Why would you covet what someone else has when you have Me?"

"Seek Me first."

"Put Me first."

"Value the treasure of relationship with Me above all, and just watch what I do *in* you, *for* you, and *through* you."

Here's the little-known secret that I need you to understand. Contentment isn't tied to your external circumstances. It's a condition of your heart. You can be in difficult circumstances and still be content. You can be in a less-than-ideal job situation and still have contentment. You can be driving a fifteen-year-old Ford station wagon with 150,000 miles on it and still be content because you have an ongoing, vital, passionate, head-over-heels relationship with Jesus Christ.

Yes, contentment is a source of great gain for two reasons. First, because it frees God to move into your circumstances and change them for the better. But more importantly, contentment positions you for a life of eternal significance and impact. That's a life that lays up great treasure in heaven, where neither rust, nor decay, nor moths, nor time can degrade your joy.

A heart of contentment is a major foundation for a life of wise stewardship.

CHAPTER TEN

THE WITNESS STAND

I was in the slow lane of a major Dallas-area freeway when I saw him coming in my rearview mirror. The car was a fairly recent model, but even at a distance I could tell it was in rough shape. It had several unrepaired dents, a cracked windshield, and it looked like it hadn't been washed in... well, ever. What got my attention was the way it was being driven—by that I mean like a crazy person was behind the wheel. It was passing cars on both the left and right—cutting several of them off and forcing them to hit their brakes.

By the time he (or she—I couldn't be sure through the dirty windshield) reached me, I was on high alert for any possibility. The car went whizzing by on my left and that's when I saw it. My heart sank, and a wave of sadness and anger swept over me.

The back side of the car prominently displayed a "Jesus fish" magnet and a peeling bumper sticker that warned the world that this car would be "unoccupied in the event of Rapture." I recall thinking, "Hey, friend, if you're going to drive like a lunatic, please, for the sake of the gospel, take the Jesus paraphernalia off your car!"

I was troubled by this seemingly minor event for two related reasons. First, this person was publicly identifying himself as a follower of Jesus Christ while being dangerous and obnoxious on the freeway.

The second and less obvious reason it bothered me was related to the condition of this individual's car. As I mentioned, it wasn't a particularly old vehicle. But the person driving it clearly didn't care about its condition or appearance. Gauging by the rust, the damage had clearly gone unrepaired for some time. And anyone with a garden hose or a few quarters can wash a car periodically. I was grieved to see a rolling public display of poor stewardship by someone advertising his affiliation with the cause of Christ.

Don't get me wrong: There is no shame in driving an older vehicle. On the contrary, I've already mentioned that we happily drove older, high-mileage cars for years as we were learning to live within our means. In fact, driving an older, paid-for car is frequently the mark of a wise steward. No, I'm talking about the message it sends to others when we clearly neglect the care and maintenance of the things God has entrusted to us. Our cars may have been old but they were always clean and in good repair. We viewed this as a fundamental part of being a good steward. But we also saw it as a part of being a good *witness*. Here's what I mean by that.

Once we're adopted into God's family—once we take the name and identity of Jesus, operating as His ambassadors to a lost and dying world—it instantly begins to matter how we present ourselves to the lost folks around us. Jesus clearly had this responsibility in mind when He

> Once we're adopted into God's family, it instantly begins to matter how we present ourselves to the lost folks around us.

said, "Let your light so shine before men, that they may see your good works and glorify your Father in heaven" (Matt. 5:16). Jesus was keenly aware that the world is watching how His people live their lives.

Have you ever noticed how often God's Word points us to our responsibilities to our "neighbor"? Several of the Ten Commandments mention the way we treat or behave toward our neighbor. Many of the other Levitical laws dealt with how to live righteously and justly with your neighbor. This carried right over into the New Testament as Jesus taught the principle of loving "your neighbor as yourself" (Matt. 22:39). This should prompt the question, Why is God so concerned about our neighbors? I believe I have an answer.

He is not ultimately interested in how you treat your neighbors. He is interested in *family*. You see, when God looks at the people around you, He doesn't see people you just happen to rub shoulders with on a regular basis. He sees prospective children. He sees people for whom Jesus died so they can be adopted back into relationship with the Father who loves them that much.

When you moved into your current neighborhood, God got excited. He looked at all the lost people that you would be encountering every day and said, "Great! Now I've got someone close enough to touch them with My love!" He saw every one of your neighbors currently living in darkness and said, "I'm so happy I'm putting a source of My light right in the middle of them." This is why the Word has so much to say about how you conduct yourself with your neighbors.

Of course, you may be wondering who is and isn't your neighbor. That's exactly what a Jewish legal expert asked Jesus one day. This man wanted Jesus to give him a clear definition of who his neighbor was so he could be sure he was technically following the law.

And behold, a certain lawyer stood up and tested Him, saying, "Teacher, what shall I do to inherit eternal life?"

He said to him, "What is written in the law? What is your reading of it?"

So he answered and said, " 'You shall love the LORD your God with all your heart, with all your soul, with all your strength, and with all your mind,' and 'your neighbor as yourself.' "

And He said to him, "You have answered rightly; do this and you will live."

But he, wanting to justify himself, said to Jesus, "And who is my neighbor?" (Luke 10:25–29)

In response to that final question, Jesus chose not to give a direct answer. Instead He told the familiar story of the "Good Samaritan"—a parable of a man who is beaten, robbed, and left for dead by the side of the road. You know the story. Several different types of people pass by the man without stopping to help him. Finally, a despised Samaritan goes far out of his way to help.

So, what was the answer to the legal expert's question embedded in Jesus' parable?

Jesus' story reveals that your "neighbor" is anyone you happen to come into contact with in your daily life. (Even on the freeway!) This certainly includes the people who live near you, but also your coworkers, your acquaintances, the people you routinely bump into at the dry cleaners, and the other parents you sit by in the stands at the soccer tournaments. But Jesus' parable also extends the definition of

> Your "neighbor" is anyone you happen to come into contact with in your daily life.

neighbor to the chance encounter at the checkout line at the grocery store. So the question becomes, What kind of story is your life telling to those with whom you interact each day?' For good or bad, your life witnesses to your neighbors in many ways.

One of the most overlooked of these is the way you handle your money and the resources God has entrusted to you.

The Quality of Your Stewardship Testifies

It's a sobering thing to think about, but when the people around you know you are a believer, the way you manage your finances witnesses to them about God. That's right—your stewardship testifies!

Don't misunderstand: I'm not talking about your level of affluence or wealth. I'm not suggesting that having nice, new things is a good advertisement for God, or that living simply and humbly is a bad one. (Although I've heard that preached and taught in the past, sadly.) No, I'm saying that the way we choose to spend our money, the wisdom with which we manage it, and the way we care for the things God has entrusted to us wordlessly *speaks* about our God to the people around us who don't know Him. Unless you're living as a hermit in the desert like an ascetic monk, you live each day on an invisible witness stand giving testimony to everyone you encounter about what it means to be a follower of Jesus Christ and a child of God.

My point is that we have a higher motivation for good stewardship than just our own personal peace and well-being. The eternal destinies of others may very well hang in the balance based on the way we represent what a Christian looks like, and how a Christian lives.

For the believer who is a chronically bad steward, that testimony is not positive. His "neighbors" are likely observing it and saying things to themselves like:

"Why would I want to be a Christian? That guy can't even pay his bills."

"Have you noticed that couple just seems to go from money crisis to money crisis? They're always so stressed out and grim."

"I wish those people down the street who are always talking about their church would either take care of their lawn and landscaping or move."

"How is it that guy always seems to be driving a new car but can't get his house painted? It's the eyesore of the block."

As with the crazy driver sporting a Jesus fish, I'm sometimes tempted to gently tell believers, "If you're going to steward your resources in such a way that your financial life is a constant train wreck, maybe keep your Christianity to yourself." Of course, I don't actually say that, but it crosses my mind. Why? Because it's just a horrible witness when we don't handle our finances wisely. When we can't pay our bills, or properly take care of our homes and cars, what kind of a testimony is that about God?

Of course, when some believers who have struggled for a long time hear this message, their impulse is to point a finger at God: *If God would increase our income, we wouldn't have these problems. God isn't providing like He promised!*

I pointed out in a previous chapter that this is a fallacy. It's a lie of Mammon. More money is not the solution. If I can't pay my bills, my problem is not that God is not providing adequately. My problem is

> If I can't pay my bills, my problem is not that God is not providing adequately. My problem is that I am not wisely managing what He is providing.

that I am not wisely managing what He is providing. That's the problem. And as we've seen, we're not likely to see more until we're being faithful and wise with what we currently have.

In contrast, when you manage your finances wisely—even if that means driving older cars, splitting an entrée at the restaurant, skipping the daily four-dollar liquid dessert at the corner coffee shop, and just generally living a simpler lifestyle—the peace and power that shine through your life reflect positively on the cause of Christ. The people you encounter in your daily life will see a person who exudes genuine peace and contentment. When they discover that you're a follower of Jesus, they'll be more inclined to want to know more about the lifestyle that can produce that kind of joy.

Joy should be the telltale hallmark of the Christian life. God wired us for joy. But few things will drive happiness from your life so completely like the chronic mismanagement of money. In fact, it will cause you to miss out on one of the greatest joys available to the believer. Allow me to explain.

Testifying Through Generosity

As we've seen, how you manage your finances and care for your assets speaks loudly and clearly to everyone around you. Your life testifies constantly—for better or worse—about what it means to be a Christian. But there is another thing that good stewardship empowers you to do that speaks even louder about the goodness of God. In fact, it shouts that our God is loving and kind and wonderful. What's more, it brings you one of the greatest thrills you can experience this side of heaven.

The reason why this is so is hidden in a very familiar little Scripture. The apostle Paul said,

Remember the words of the Lord Jesus, that He said, "It is more blessed to give than to receive." (Acts 20:35)

Did you know the Greek word translated as "blessed" in that verse (*makarios*) simply means "happy"? That means a fair paraphrase of that verse would be, "People who give are happier than those who receive." Much of my previous book, *The Blessed Life*, was built around the truth that a life of generosity is a happy life. Indeed, based on what I just told you about the word *makarios*, I could just as easily have titled it *The Happy Life*. And with good reason! At the root of that book's premise lies the truth that the happiest, most fulfilling, most joy-filled life you can experience is a life of generosity.

Yet as I pointed out in the opening pages of *this* book, it's impossible to be as generous as you'd like to be when you're living under financial pressure, spending more than you make, or buried in debt. As I also pointed out, the moment you take a step of faith to become a good steward, the power of God comes rushing in to help you, meeting your diligent efforts with miracles of provision and promotion.

Here is my point. Yes, our good stewardship testifies of God's goodness to those you encounter in your daily life, but it does something else quite wonderful. Good stewardship gives you the financial margin to be generous and give to others as the Spirit of God prompts you. That's where the real fun starts. There are few things more gratifying or exciting than getting the opportunity to be a miraculous manifestation of God's goodness and love to someone who isn't expecting it. Allow me to share just one example from my own life.

Several summers ago, Debbie and I took a long-awaited vacation to New Mexico by motorcycle. I put her on the back of my big cruising bike and we headed for the mountains—away from the stifling Texas heat. The plan was for our grown, married children to fly up and join us later in the trip.

One particular day we were enjoying riding the twisting roads in the crisp mountain air when we pulled over to a little roadside café to grab some lunch. Now, as it happened, I was carrying an unusually large sum of money in cash. Why? Out of habit, really. Early in our marriage, we didn't carry credit cards. As I've mentioned previously, one of our key stewardship disciplines was to pay cash for everything. That meant when we'd saved up enough money to take a vacation, I brought the vacation budget with me in cash! That way, we never accidentally spent more than we intended. The budget for the vacation was in my pocket. (We'll talk about budgeting in chapter 13.) Well, over the years we started carrying credit cards and using them judiciously, always paying them off fully each month and never having credit card debt. (We'll talk about how to do that in chapter 14.) Over the years I'd gotten so accustomed to having a lot of cash with me on vacation that, for no real logical reason, I withdrew a fairly large sum right before we left on our trip—this, even though I'd planned on putting most of our vacation expenses on a credit card (for points!) and then paying the balance off in full when we got home. I actually remember telling God early in the trip, "Lord, I really don't know why I brought all this money with me. Old habits die hard, I guess!" I laughed out loud about it at the time.

So, on that beautiful day, Debbie and I found ourselves walking into that Colorado roadside diner dressed in our full motorcycling gear. We were both wearing leather head to toe, had motorcycle helmets under our arms, and I hadn't shaved in several days. Now, I doubt anyone mistook us for members of Hells Angels, but they probably wouldn't have guessed "preacher and preacher's wife," either.

As we were sitting there enjoying each other's company and the view out the window, we watched a family climb out of an older minivan, come in, and fill a table not far from where we were sitting. The father, mother, and four kids of varying ages all had the look of being on vacation, too. Now, Debbie and I are people watchers. I noticed that their kids were polite and well behaved. We also soon noticed this mother and father adding up the cost of the menu items they were considering. We heard them talking about several of them sharing meals to save on costs and stay within their budget. The scene instantly took me back to the days when our kids were small and Debbie and I were finding every way we could to save nickels, spend wisely, and never waste a thing. Splitting entrées was our signature move for the first several years of our marriage.

Suddenly I heard the familiar voice of my heavenly Father. *Now you know why you brought all that cash.*

We watched them a little while longer. When their food arrived, we watched six heads bow to give thanks.

I looked at Debbie and said, "Honey, I feel like we're supposed to bless that family."

She said, "Yes, I've been watching them, too. I agree. You want to pay for their meal?"

"Well, actually I want to pay for their vacation."

I went on to explain that I felt the Lord wanted me to give them all the cash in my wallet, and that it was quite a bit of money. And that if we did end up needing some cash later on, we could get some more.

"That's great! Go for it!" Debbie said. My sweet wife is always as eager to bless other people as I am, if not more so.

A few minutes later this family looked startled, puzzled, and maybe a little alarmed when a scruffy leather-clad biker man walked up to their table and started talking to them. I can't recall exactly what I said, but it was something along the lines of, "I'm a Christian and I always try to obey what God tells me to do." They looked even more puzzled when I laid a fairly thick stack of bills on the table and said, "God wants to pay for your vacation."

Frankly, it was hard to get them to receive it at first. I think initially they thought I was trying to involve them in some sort of illegal activity. Life in this world had taught them that there had to be a catch. Random strangers don't just walk up to you and hand you a stack of cash. But one did that day. Because God loves people. And He needs His people to express and manifest that love to them.

Eventually it sank in and they received the gift with wonder and gratitude. Before I stepped away, I looked at the kids and said, "Please always remember this day. Never forget the day that God told a stranger in a restaurant to pay for your vacation because He loves you and cares about you."

Now, this was on the front end of a three-week getaway. Before long our kids and their spouses joined us as we all stayed together in a mountain lodge near Red River, New Mexico. There was golf, hiking, river floats, great food; and lots of other fun activities.

My point is that although we had many wonderful moments on that trip, not one of them compared to that moment in that diner. If Debbie and I live to be 110, we'll remember and treasure that memory and feel the joy of being in a position to manifest the true nature of our wonderful God to a struggling family. But we could only do it because we had it to give.

The Bible is true. It really is a happier thing to give than to receive. God wired you for joy, but if you don't manage your finances, you are missing out on a lot of it. You're missing out on hope. You're missing out on some amazing things God wants you to experience.

> God wired you for joy.

The greatest of these experiences is the opportunity to be a living, breathing, flesh-and-blood manifestation of God's love to another person. That's real joy. That's a happy life.

Testify

Like it or not, you're on the witness stand today. You're up there every day. Your life is testifying to a watching world about the nature of the God you serve and the Jesus who gave His life as a sacrifice to save yours. This is why the quality of your stewardship is so important. And it's why it's so vital to get to a place where you can get in on the fun of serving, helping, and blessing others. Remember Jesus's words: "Let your light so shine before men, that they may see *your good works* and glorify your Father…" (Matt. 5:16, emphasis added)

Don't misunderstand. Your "good works" have no bearing on your salvation or how much God loves you. But your good works do have an impact on others. They shine as a light for people in darkness. Your generosity points them to God and helps them understand that He is wonderfully, gloriously good.

This isn't the only reason to ask God to help you become a better steward—but it's a mighty good one. In the next section, we'll dive into the nitty-gritty of that process. Let's now explore the practical steps that take you to a life beyond blessed!

CHAPTER ELEVEN

AIM BEFORE YOU SHOOT

It was my seventh-grade year. I was taller than the average guy in my class and also afflicted with an excess of self-confidence. So I decided to go out for the basketball team. In my mind, my basketball skills—honed to a fine edge via an occasional game of H.O.R.S.E. at a neighbor's driveway hoop—were world-class. As the first day of practice approached, I couldn't wait to get out there so I could show the coach and the other kids what I could do.

At that first practice, after a few warm-ups, it was time for our first skills drill. We were told to line up at the half-court line for layups. I sprinted to be the first in line. With my vivid imagination, I had already envisioned how it was going to go. I was going to drive to the basket and execute a perfect layup with the ball gracefully arcing toward the backboard and then through the net. At that point, the coach would stop the next boy from going, gather the guys around, and say, "Did you boys see that? I really hope you were watching carefully because *that* is how a layup is done. That was a textbook layup. Perfect. If you want to be a good basketball player, do all your layups exactly like this boy did his." Then, getting a little choked up, he'd say, "In twenty years of coaching the game of basketball, I've never seen a display of natural talent like this." And then the rest of the guys would nod their heads in admiring approval.

I was so sure that was the way it was going to transpire that I made sure I was first to go. A quick chirp of Coach's whistle signaled me to begin my demonstration. I took off down the court, and before I even got to the free-throw line, he blew his whistle again and said, "Stop!" I thought, *Wow, I was so good he didn't even need to see me shoot!*

I heard Coach say, "Come on back here and start again." Then he turned to the guys in line and said, "Now, I want you guys to watch closely here."

Here we go! It's happening!

So I took off again, this time with a little more swagger and style in my step. Once again, about the time I got to the free-throw line, he blew his whistle and yelled, "Stop!" Then he turned to the guys and said, "Now, somebody tell me... Where was he looking while he was dribbling?"

A chorus of voices said, "The ball!"

At that point, I thought I was about to be praised for my intense focus and concentration. But then I heard, "Son, look at me." The tone of his voice didn't sound like one of a man about to deliver a rousing commendation. Then he pointed toward the basket and said, "*That* is the goal. You will never make a goal if you're looking at the ball."

Wait... what?

"You're going to have to learn to dribble without looking at the ball," he continued. "You have to look at the goal. You're never going to be a good basketball player unless you learn to keep your eyes forward. Now, go to the back of the line. Who's next?"

Although my pride was badly wounded, it was my dream of professional sports stardom that suffered a fatal injury on the court that day. It wasn't a total disaster, however. I did come away with a useful life principle—namely, that if I want to arrive at a goal, I need to keep it in front of me and my eyes on it.

My son James learned the same principle in a different context when he was a younger man. He had acquired his first motorcycle and was taking a basic motorcycle safety class. One of the first lessons in the class was on turning. The first thing the teacher taught them was, "Look where you *want* to go, not where you're currently going."

This is counterintuitive for most of us, and it definitely was for James. If he needed to steer around a pothole or an orange traffic cone, his natural tendency was to focus on the obstacle rather than the pathway around the obstacle. The problem is, as any experienced motorcyclist will tell you, the bike naturally goes where you're looking. James wanted to take good care of his shiny new mode of transportation, so the last thing he wanted to do was risk damaging it by hitting a big pothole. Yet while driving he would see a big crater in the road and think to himself, "Pothole. Don't hit that pothole. Yep, that pothole right up there. That's the pothole I want to avoid. That big, deep pothole." *Ka-thunk!*

He hit several potholes, oil slicks, and dead possums before he was able to train his eyes and mind to ignore the obstacle and focus on the goal—the route around it. What the

> Choose a point in the distance that will lead you away from danger and focus your eyes on that point.

instructor had taught him is amazingly effective—that is, to choose a point in the distance that will lead you away from danger and focus your eyes on that point.

The fact is we all unthinkingly steer toward the thing we're focused on, whether we want to go there or not. Highway patrol troopers and roadside construction crews are keenly aware of this phenomenon. Every year law enforcement personnel and construction workers are injured or worse because drivers plow into them while they're standing on the shoulder. Sometimes this is the result of a driver dozing off. But in many cases the driver was alert and looking directly at the flashing warning lights. Indeed, they were so focused on them that they unwittingly veered right toward them.

We naturally move toward the point of our focus.

All these illustrations point us to a very biblical truth: A focus on goals is a vital key to getting where we want to go in life and in God. If your desired destination is a lifestyle of peace and power resulting from living within your means, freedom from debt, and joyful generosity, then you'll need some specific goals on which to focus. Former secretary of state Henry Kissinger once said, "If you don't know where you are going, every road will lead you nowhere." Let's explore that truth.

Eyes on the Prize

Start talking about goal setting in our jaded, cynical, postmodern culture and eyes begin to roll. To modern ears, encouragement to write down goals can sound like a corny, old-school cliché. Something only motivational speakers used to mention during positive-thinking sales seminars. That's unfortunate because there is great power in setting tangible, measurable, achievable goals. It's a very biblical practice we see mentioned directly or implied throughout Scripture.

Paul clearly had this principle in mind when he told this to the church in Philippi:

> Not that I have already attained, or am already perfected; but I press on, that I may lay hold of that for which Christ Jesus has also laid hold of me. Brethren, I do not count myself to have apprehended; but one thing I do, forgetting those things which are behind and reaching forward to those things which are ahead, *I press toward the goal for the prize* of the upward call of God in Christ Jesus. (Philippians 3:12–14, emphasis added)

Isn't Paul essentially saying that he's doing precisely what my seventh-grade basketball coach and James' motorcycle safety instructor both recommended? He's not looking back or around. Paul has identified his objective and is keeping his eyes forward-looking and his focus on "the goal for the prize." Paul knew what many people today do not—namely, that there is tremendous power in setting a goal and creating an actionable plan to achieve it.

As Solomon advised his son, "Commit to the LORD whatever you do, and he will establish your plans" (Prov. 16:3 NIV), and, "Where there is no vision, the people perish" (Prov. 29:18 KJV).

Of course, it's not just the Bible that suggests that goal setting helps us get where we want to go and achieve what we hope to accomplish.

> Setting measurable goals is powerful—particularly when those goals are written down.

The evidence from the worlds of business and behavioral science is overwhelming. Countless anecdotes and studies reveal that setting measurable goals is powerful—particularly when those goals are written down.

For example, a rigorous long-term study conducted at California's Dominican University revealed that individuals who wrote down specific goals were significantly more likely to achieve those goals than those who merely thought about them without writing them down.[1] This same study went further in that it also evaluated the effect of creating an action plan for achieving those goals. Not surprisingly, among those who wrote down their goals, those who added a plan of action were even more successful over time.[2] This research didn't stop there. It also tracked the progress of a group that also created regular points of accountability for their plan. In other words, one subset of the individuals in the study not only wrote down their goals and crafted a step-by-step plan of action for achieving them, but they also gave key people in their lives visibility of those plans and asked them to hold them accountable to following them. This added ingredient of regular accountability made this group the most successful of all in reaching their objectives.[3]

Other studies have validated these results. Add to this the testimonies of countless high achievers and successful individuals who attest to the power of writing down specific goals and then crafting an action plan for achieving them. My friend Rick Warren, pastor of Saddleback Church and author of *The Purpose Driven Life*, is among them. Rick has written,

Research has revealed that people have more difficulty setting goals than they do accomplishing them once they are set. The hardest part for most of us is sitting down and thinking about what God wants us to do in our lives. As pastors, we struggle to find time to plan and just think.

An interesting national survey a few years ago showed that the biggest difference between moderately successful people and highly successful people is that the second group wrote down their goals. In just about every other area—education, ability, talent, etc.—they were equals. What's true of the general population is also true of us in ministry. Those who set goals in ministry are typically the ones who succeed.[4]

My personal observations and experience agree with Rick's. So let's now apply these principles to the theme and focus of this book—that is, getting you to a place in which you're living a life beyond blessed through wise stewardship.

Where Are You?

Before you can figure out where you want to go, you need a clear understanding of where you are. If you're going to set a goal to walk to Denver, you need to know which direction from Denver you currently are, and how far away it is.

In a similar way, if your goal is to be debt-free, it's vital to know precisely how much debt you currently have. I'm consistently stunned to encounter believers who wish they were debt-free but don't have a clear idea of how deep a hole they're actually in. I say "wish" because if you don't even know how much debt you have, you can't really call it a "goal" to be debt-free. However, it's not enough to just add up the balances on all your debts.

To craft an achievable goal and actionable strategy for eliminating it, you really need to know the type of debt each obligation represents (secured, unsecured, mortgage, student loan, etc.). You also need to know the interest rate, the minimum payment, and the remaining term of each obligation. If you have basic spreadsheet skills, it's a great way to compile all this information. But a simple legal pad will do the job as well. The important things are to be able to see your total indebtedness and to know which debts are carrying the highest interest rates. For a goal related to debt reduction or debt elimination, this sheet tells you "where you are."

You'll utilize a similar process for any other financial goals you might set—whether it's reducing your monthly expenses, saving for a down payment on a home, or funding the adoption of a child from another country.

You're only wandering aimlessly if you don't really know where you are. Once you have a clear grasp of your situation, then you're ready for the next step.

Where Do You Want to Go?

Once you've had a clear-eyed look at your current situation, you're ready to get down to the business of setting your financial goals. Here are a few wisdom principles

First of all...pray!

and tips for navigating this part of the process.

First of all...pray! Ask the Spirit of God for clarity of vision and purpose so you can aim at the right target or targets. So often we attack the wrong thing first, or go after a symptom instead of an underlying cause of our problems. Many people hack wildly at the branches of the thing that is creating chaos in their lives when one concentrated blow at the root would yield the results they're looking for. Ask for and receive wisdom. Embrace both the promise and warning we find in James 1:5–6:

If any of you lacks wisdom, let him ask of God, who gives to all liberally and without reproach, and it will be given to him. But let him ask in faith, with no doubting, for he who doubts is like a wave of the sea driven and tossed by the wind.

You're not on your own here! God is your eager and powerful partner in this endeavor to align your life with His wisdom and ways. Involve Him in every facet.

Secondly, don't set goals to impress others, or be pressured into goals that are based on someone else's values. Pursuing a goal to completion will require perseverance, passion, and the drive to press through adversity and discouragement. If a goal doesn't spring from your heart and vision (and that of your spouse if you're married), you'll run out of steam when the going gets tough. The most important aspect of a goal you'll actually achieve is that it is *your* goal.

Thirdly, an effective goal must be specific and measurable. A desire to "be a better person" isn't really a goal. It's more of a sentiment. The same for a goal like "Get in better shape." How do you plan to measure that? How will you know that you're making progress and that you've arrived? Of course, financial goals tend to be easier to measure. Usually there are numbers associated with the objectives. If your goal is to reduce your monthly spending to a certain point below your monthly income, simple math will tell you where you are, where you need to be, and what the distance is between those two points. There is a clear way to measure that objective.

Well-crafted goals are also very specific. The more specific the goal, the more power to pull you forward it contains. Vague, fuzzy goals are rarely compelling goals. A fuzzy goal is "Reduce my debt burden." How much lower? What kind of debt? A better one would be "Eliminate all credit card debt by July Fourth of next year."

Jack Canfield, cocreator of the *Chicken Soup for the Soul* books, summarizes this kind of specificity by simply asking, "How much, by when?" He writes,

[A goal] must meet two criteria. It must be stated in a way that you and anybody else could measure it. *I will lose 10 pounds* is not as powerful as *I will weigh 135 pounds by 5 o'clock on June 30.* The second is clearer, because anybody can show up at 5 o'clock on June 30 and look at the reading on your scale.[5]

As a very young adult, my son James had a wise mentor who challenged him to pray and think about his short-term, medium-term, and long-term goals for his life, and to write them down. He will admit that he was completely stumped at first. Goal-oriented thinking simply doesn't come naturally to many of us. It has to be learned. He didn't even know where to start.

His life coach wisely encouraged him to be very specific in articulating his goals. He will tell you it was a painful process that at times almost seemed like a punishment. But he will also tell you that it refined and clarified his sense of purpose, helped him make better choices, fueled his focus, and fed his determination. Over the years his goals have evolved and changed, which is a normal part of maturing, but what has remained is the skill and habit of being goal oriented.

Crafting your goals in this way greatly enhances your prospects for reaching them. As the world-famous Christian motivational author and speaker Zig Ziglar has said, "A goal properly set is half-way reached."[6]

How Long Will It Take to Get There?

Finally, goals should be ambitious enough to challenge you, but they should also be attainable. If you're facing a mountain of credit card debt you spent the last five years piling up, a goal such as "We will be free of all credit card debt in three months" is both specific and measurable but may be too aggressive to be attainable. Yes, God is going to assist and bless you in many ways as you pursue your goals. You can be sure of that. But setting a goal that requires nothing short of a miracle to achieve isn't really a goal. That's a prayer of desperation. Of course, prayer is a wonderful thing. And God does indeed bring about miracles for His children. But that's not what we're talking about here. There is no possible plan of action you can put in place for a goal that can only be accomplished by a major miracle. Your plan is little more than "Wait and hope for God to do something spectacular."

There is a difference between childlike faith and arrogant presumption. Set your goal within a time frame that is reasonably achievable through diligence and consistency; then don't be surprised if God rewards your diligence by miraculously accelerating your progress!

Certainly, if you are facing what seems like an insurmountable mountain, it can be daunting and more than a little discouraging to look at a long timeline before you reach the promised land of achievement. That's why it's wise to break big goals up into smaller, incremental goals. The standard answer to the age-old question, "How do you eat an elephant?" remains unchanged. "One bite at a time."

When faced with a long voyage, the wise traveler breaks the journey up into smaller chunks at established waypoints or milestones to mark his or her progress. In a similar way, it's helpful to break your biggest, most ambitious goals down into incremental steps. Mark Twain is reported to have said, "The secret of getting ahead is getting started. The secret of getting started is breaking your complex, overwhelming tasks into small manageable tasks, and then starting on the first one."[7]

> Break your biggest, most ambitious goals down into incremental steps.

Write the Vision

As the goal-setting study from Dominican University revealed, people who write down their goals are much more likely to follow them through to completion. There is seemingly supernatural power in the act of writing a goal down. Something about it moves it from the realm of mere thought into the material realm where we live and act.

So once you (and your spouse if you're married) have arrived at your financial goals, write them down! I would encourage you to also make copies and put them in places where you'll see them regularly. Otherwise, if they're out of sight, they're out of mind. Put them in your Bible or journal, on your bathroom mirror, or on the refrigerator. Make them the screen saver on your smartphone. In fact, it wouldn't be a bad idea to write down your biggest financial goal on a card and place it in your wallet or pocketbook. Place it where every time you reach in your wallet to grab a credit or debit card, you'll see it and remember what you're working and praying for. Be like Paul and keep your focus on "the goal for the prize." In this case, the prize is the peace and freedom you'll experience when you have moved into the land of good stewardship. The prize is the lifestyle of joy you'll live when you can be generous and bless others every time the Spirit of God prompts you.

Keep your goals before your eyes every day and your chances of achieving them will go way up.

Make an Action Plan

A second important takeaway from the Dominican study was that adding a plan of action for achieving your written goals boosts your odds of success even further. "Plan your work and then work your plan," the old saying goes.

It's true. Once you know where you are, where you want to go, and roughly how great the distance is between those two points, it's important to craft a practical, workable strategy for making regular progress in that direction. What that plan looks like is determined by the nature of the goal.

I know a couple who found themselves with a handful of maxed-out credit cards after the husband lost his job and didn't find a new one for more than eighteen months. They began by agreeing on the goal of paying off every penny of that high-interest debt and asking for God's help. Their next step was to determine how low they could reduce their monthly expenses in order to free up as much money as possible with which to attack these balances. They continued to put God first with their tithe so the rest of their income would be blessed. As a result, they determined that it would require two years of diligence to get all the balances to zero. Thus, their stated goal became, "We will be free of all credit card debt this date (two years from now)."

In addition to having a specific, measurable goal, they had a plan that included paying the minimums on the cards with lower interest rates and throwing everything else they had at the card with the highest interest rate. When that balance was paid in full, they would then focus on the card with the next-highest rate, and so on.

As it happened, several months into the effort, he got a raise. (Imagine that!) And because they were passionate and focused on their goal, they used every bit of the additional income (after their tithe) to accelerate their plan. God also gave them other opportunities to earn additional income. Out of the blue something would come along that would add momentum to their debt reduction program. In the end, what had originally been estimated to require twenty-four months only took sixteen! God had noted their diligence and heart for good stewardship, rewarding it with supernatural help and blessing.

My point is, add a practical plan for reaching your incremental subgoals and your overall objective. Once you have a strategy, stick to it with bulldog-like tenacity. There is power in consistency.

Add Accountability and Assistance

Finally, the Dominican study also revealed the power of adding a layer of accountability to your goal setting and planning. There is great wisdom in having a person or persons outside your household who know what you've committed to do and what your plan is. (This is what my son James did by acquiring a mentor who held him accountable to the goals that he'd set.) Such a person should be invited and empowered to check in with you regularly to monitor your progress. Often just knowing that someone else is going to be asking about your efforts can keep you disciplined and diligent.

Of course, this requires transparency and vulnerability on your part. That makes trustworthiness a vital attribute of your accountability team. Ideally these people will be wise, mature, insightful individuals who can offer you advice as well as encouragement.

Most believers who are struggling in some area of their lives—especially their finances—never ask for help. Why? Well, do you remember the story of my basketball debut I shared at the beginning of this chapter? I can joke about it now, but that was a very humiliating experience for me. Most people don't seek help because they fear something similar. We're ashamed. Shame about the condition of your finances will keep you from getting the very help and encouragement that will turn your situation around.

When you're sick, you go to a doctor. If your finances are sick, go talk to someone trustworthy and knowledgeable who can help you diagnose the root problem and prescribe the right course of action. This is *very* important! Please avail yourself of the many Christian

> See a financial "doctor" and follow the prescription!

stewardship ministries that are available. See a financial "doctor" and follow the prescription! Don't let pride or fear keep you from straightening out this area of your life. It's too important. Your peace and health are at stake. Your marriage is at stake. Your children's futures are at stake.

Harness the power of goal setting to get healthy in every area of your life.

CHAPTER TWELVE

HEARSES DON'T PULL U-HAULS

Readers above a certain age will remember a beloved radio personality named Paul Harvey, a fixture on our nation's AM radio stations throughout the seventies, eighties, and nineties. Mr. Harvey used to have a daily two-minute feature called *The Rest of the Story*. In it he would reveal a surprising, little-known backstory of a famous person or event. He'd close each episode with the phrase that became his calling card. "And now you know... the *rest* of the story!"

Well, for readers of my first book, *The Blessed Life*, I have an important backstory for you. In that book I shared a bit of the remarkable stewardship testimony of a good friend of mine. If you haven't yet read *The Blessed Life*, here's what I shared:

I have a friend who, years ago, was making $37,500. At that time, he was consistently giving 10 percent of his gross income. Then the Lord spoke to him and said, "I want you to give 15 percent; and if you will give 15 percent this year, I'll double your income; and, by the way, if you'll give 20 percent the next year, I'll double it again; and if you'll give 25 percent in the year after that, I'll double it again." He felt very strongly that the Lord had spoken this to his heart.

He did not come back at God and say, "How about this? You double my income, and then I'll start giving 15 percent."

He took God at His Word and seized the opportunity to stretch his faith and please God. Right away, he started giving 15 percent of his income to the work of the Lord. That year, his income went from $37,500 to $75,000. Taking the Lord at His Word once again, he started giving 20 percent. That following year, he made $150,000. It was at this point that I met him for the first time. We became good friends, and he related this testimony to me.

The next year, he upped his giving to 25 percent, and his income rose to $300,000. I know it sounds incredible, but I know this testimony to be true. This man is a dear friend of mine.

The year after he upped his giving to 30 percent, he made $600,000. A year later, he upped it to 35 percent and grossed $1.2 million. Until he sold his business in 2010, he consistently gave over 50 percent of his income to the work of God. Now that he is in full-time ministry, he is still giving 30 to 35 percent each year.

But can I tell you that the greatest thing about this testimony is not how much money my friend gives or makes; it's what God has done in his heart.

This is a man of God. He didn't start giving out of a desire to be rich. He obeyed out of a heart to please God and be used by Him.

God looked down and said, "I need to distribute funds in My kingdom, and here's someone I can trust." And that's precisely what He's looking for. God is looking for people He can trust with wealth.[1]

At his request, I didn't mention my friend's name in *The Blessed Life*, but he has now given me permission to "out" him, in part because he has since sold his business and is now a full-time member of the pastoral staff of Gateway Church. His name is Steve Dulin, and every word of that testimony is true. However, it is not the whole picture. It's time for you to hear "the rest of the story."

The fact is that when God spoke to Steve and his wife, Melody, a few years before I met them, Steve was just starting out in the construction business. He wasn't making a lot of money and they were carrying some low-interest student loan debt as well as a mortgage on their modest home. It was then the Lord actually gave him not one but *three* directives concerning his finances. Yes, the Lord challenged him to increase his giving above his tithe in the way I described in *The Blessed Life*. And those were indeed the astounding results he experienced. But at the same time God told him to increase his giving, He also told him to get out of debt and start saving more. That's right. At the very same time the Lord instructed Steve to start giving more to the work of the kingdom, He also told him to eliminate his debt and to start building up his savings! How's that for a challenge!

Of course, those directives came with a promise. Yet it was not the promise of increased income that moved this couple to step out in faith. It was their heart to obey what God had told them to do. It would be appropriate to point out here that I'm not recommending that you try

> There are always good things waiting on the other side of obedience to God's directives.

to replicate exactly what Steve did. There was power and blessing in it because it was what God instructed them to do. There are always good things waiting on the other side of obedience to God's directives.

However, you will recall that back in chapter 4 I made the statement that good stewards do three things: They (1) spend wisely, (2) save, and (3) give. If you understand that a key element of "spending wisely" is not carrying unsecured debt, you'll see that God's instructions to Steve were pretty much a road map for good stewardship. Aggressively good stewardship! (We'll discuss the use of debt in chapter 14.)

The Dulins stepped out in obedience and immediately adjusted their lifestyle and budget so they could increase their giving, accelerate their payments on their student loans, and start putting money away in savings. As we've seen with several of the testimonies I've shared so far, this step is the "secret sauce" of all financial breakthroughs. We have to be willing to make the hard choices and adjustments that will allow us to practice good stewardship.

Following this God-given road map to the letter led Steve to a counterintuitive decision. As it happened, he had enough money socked away in an investment that was returning, on average, about 8 or 9 percent per year, to completely pay off his student loans with money leftover. Meanwhile, the interest on those student loans was only 2 or 3 percent per year. Now, no financial advisor on earth would counsel someone to take money that is earning 9 percent and use it to pay off debt with a 3 percent rate. In natural terms this seemed foolish. Yet this is precisely what he did. At the time several people in his life who knew what he was doing told him it was crazy to pull that money out to pay off that loan.

Steve knew clearly what God had instructed him to do. For him, it wasn't about logic or reason. It was simply about obedience in faith. As a result, the investment account was liquidated, the school loans were paid off, and the balance of the funds was thrown at their home mortgage loan. The mortgage, too? Yes—keep in mind that God's instruction to Steve was, "Get out of debt."

Today Steve teaches that the key to high-level stewardship is seeking God and doing what He tells you to do. And in the absence of a specific word or instruction, simply follow the basic stewardship principles from God's Word that we are exploring in this book. Steve says,

> It wasn't just that we started giving more, although that was one-third of God's instruction to us. If I hadn't also been intentional about getting out of debt and saving more, I'm not sure we would have seen the miraculous increase that we saw. We can't just obey what we want to obey and ignore the rest. God gave me three things to do. So, I went and did those three things, with His help. Obedience to what God is saying is the operative principle.

Here, in practical terms, is how Steve and Melody accomplished this remarkable feat of stewardship. Putting God first, they started with their tithe, which God had told them to increase from 10 to 15 percent. Then they prayed about the amounts they were going to save and put against debt each month. In both cases, they believed God gave them a specific figure. They added these three numbers up and subtracted the total from their anticipated monthly net income. The remaining amount of money became their monthly living budget. They then set about making whatever adjustments were necessary to live on that amount.

Of course, most people today would approach this exercise from the opposite direction. With goals of giving more, saving more, and paying down debt, they would start with their living expenses. They would try to see where they could shave some costs down here and there, and then let what's leftover determine how much they could apply toward their goals. If the Dulins had approached things this way, they wouldn't have that remarkable testimony today.

Of course, as they faithfully stepped out, God did indeed meet them with His miraculous power to bring increase. Steve's construction business thrived, and the extraordinary annual doubling of their household income began. As their income increased, so did their giving, saving, and debt reduction. Within a few years, they had paid off their mortgage completely and actually paid cash for their next house.

In the years after I first shared Steve's story in *The Blessed Life*, his construction business continued to thrive and provide jobs for many people. Meanwhile, Steve and Melody continued their journey of radical stewardship. A few years ago, God stirred a new direction in Steve's heart—a call into full-time ministry. So he sold his business and joined the pastoral staff of Gateway Church.

He continues to be an amazing example of what it means to be a faithful steward, not only of money and material things, but also of his gifts, time, energy, and calling. He is a tremendous blessing to our church.

Hear, Trust, and Obey

The key to Steve Dulin's amazing stewardship testimony will also be the key to yours. (That's right—the rest of your story is waiting to be told. You are a stewardship testimony in the making.) That key? The willingness to live below your means.

It's simple. But *simple* doesn't mean easy. There is no shortcut through or bypass around this step.

I'm sorry, but you're not going to win the lottery. You don't have a wealthy elderly aunt you've never

> *Simple* doesn't mean easy.

heard of out there who is about to leave this world. You're going to have to do whatever it takes to adjust your lifestyle so that your income consistently exceeds your outgo. And the sooner you get started, the sooner you'll come out on the other side, into the land beyond blessed.

Taking this step requires trust. Trust in God's goodness and faithfulness. It means believing Him when He tells us that He will "never leave us nor forsake us." It means trusting Him to honor His promise that if we'll "seek first the kingdom of God," He will respond by adding "all these things" like food, clothing, and shelter to us. Yes, it takes trust in God to live within your means. Conversely, when you're not living within your means, you're actually demonstrating to God that you don't trust Him to meet your needs.

Please keep in mind that typical Christians living beyond their means aren't spending two to three times as much as they make. No one with a $50,000 income is tempted to try to live a $150,000 lifestyle. This destructive trap is far subtler than that. The real temptation for a person making $50,000 is to spend every bit of that and just a little bit more. As we observed previously, the seductive path is to steal from your future self.

God wants to help you do the opposite of this—to actually turn this poisonous practice on its head. I'm talking about living well *below* your means. This is precisely what Steve and Melody did, with extraordinary results. They trusted. And they obeyed.

Please note that I am encouraging you to live "well below" your means. Now, if you've been spending more than you make for some time, then reducing your outgo to 90 or 95 percent of your income is certainly a great step in the right direction. But that will not get you out of the hole you've dug for yourself. Nor will it allow you to save and give at the levels that will produce a beyond-blessed life.

Learning to live well below your means may very well be the most powerful, life-transforming, peace-bringing habit you can acquire. Yet only a tiny fraction of people do it. Let's explore a couple of common reasons for that.

Hearses and U-Hauls

Why do we find it so hard to live within our means? The answer lies in a passage we've already visited once. You'll recall that 1 Timothy 6:6 says, "Now' godliness with contentment is great gain." However, we didn't read beyond that verse previously. Let's do so now because the next one holds a pretty important truth, too. Verse 7 says, "For we brought nothing into this world, and it is certain we can carry nothing out." I have a friend who has that truth in mind when he says, "You've never seen a hearse pulling a U-Haul." It's true. Warren Buffett and Bill Gates will take the same amount of material wealth into eternity as you and I will. That is, precisely none. And yet most people spend their entire lives pursuing wealth and neglecting to store up the kind of treasure that will last for eternity. That's foolish, and indeed that's precisely what this passage goes on to say:

And having food and clothing, with these we shall be content. But those who desire to be rich fall into temptation and a snare and into many foolish and harmful lusts, which drown men in destruction and perdition. For the love of money is a root of all kinds of evil, for which some have strayed from the faith in their greediness, and pierced themselves through with many sorrows. (1 Timothy 6:8–10)

First, please note that this passage did NOT say "money is the root of all evil"—even though 99 percent of the civilized world quotes it that way. No, it is the "love of money" that the Word sternly warns us about, as well as a lust to be rich. In the earlier chapter on contentment and the Spirit of Mammon, we saw that looking to riches for happiness or a sense of significance is a form of idolatry. No wonder a lust for wealth can "drown men in destruction and perdition." That's the inevitable end result of all idol worship.

If you want to live below your means, the most important thing you can do is learn to be content. The fact is contentment is a learnable skill. Paul said so:

For *I have learned to be content* whatever the circumstances. I know what it is to be in need, and I know what it is to have plenty. I have learned the secret of being content in any and every situation, whether well fed or hungry, whether living in plenty or in want. I can do all this through him who gives me strength. (Philippians 4:11–13 NIV, emphasis added)

As we discussed previously, contentment doesn't result from having pleasant external circumstances. Most people in America have pleasant external circumstances yet they're not content at all.

> Contentment comes from within you. It's an attitude and posture of the heart.

Contentment comes from within you. It's an attitude and posture of the heart. That's why Paul said he had learned to be content in every type of situation and season of life.

Having a heart attitude of discontentment leads you to buy things you can't afford. And buying things you can't afford actually sends a message to God. You are boldly stating to your heavenly Father, "I am not satisfied with the provision You have provided me. And I'm not content with You. You're not enough to satisfy my soul." Of course, you might never be brazen enough to consciously, deliberately say such words to God. Nevertheless, when you run out and buy something with a credit card without the money to pay the balance in full by the end of the month, you are, in effect, saying, "I am not content with the way You are providing for me."

So many people today try to appear richer than they actually are. In contrast, I know many extraordinarily wealthy individuals who, if you saw them on the street or met them at a social gathering, you would never guess that they were rich. This is nothing new, however. Solomon pointed out this contrast in the book of Proverbs roughly three thousand years ago:

> There is one who pretends to be rich, but has nothing;
> another pretends to be poor, but has great wealth. (Proverbs
> 13:7 NASB)

Allow me to paraphrase Solomon: "Many of the people you're envying because they look so prosperous are actually dead broke and up to their eyeballs in debt. And some of the people around you who don't look all that impressive are actually quite wealthy, but they're good stewards, so they're secure and happy." Sam Walton was one of the richest men in the world, but he drove a 1979 Ford F-150 pickup truck until the day he died. If you'd bumped into him in the aisle of one of his Walmart stores, you would never have guessed he was a billionaire many times over.

Envy is a terribly destructive thing. When you allow the toxin of envy to live in your soul, you begin to resent others for what they have. But something even more corrosive happens in your heart. When you're an envious person, you begin to want to be envied by others. Millions of people spend money they don't have not because they truly want or need things but simply in a carnal quest to be the envy of others. In other words, to make other people feel bad about themselves. What a low and ugly motivation for living!

Yes, a lack of contentment is the primary reason people fail to live within their means. Unlike Paul, they haven't learned how to be content in every circumstance. As Paul warned Timothy, this opens the door to all kinds of evil and destruction in their lives.

Paul also mentioned greediness in that passage in I Timothy. The fact is once you start down the road of looking to things for happiness, you never actually arrive at the hoped-for destination. You'll always need more. Ecclesiastes 5:10 says, "He who loves silver will not be satisfied with silver; nor he who loves abundance, with increase." The love of money is *never* satisfied. Paul said greed will cause you to stray from the faith and end up pierced through with many sorrows.

I don't want that for you! I want you to experience the amazing lifestyle of blessing, peace, and purpose that result from being a wise steward. And that means biting the bullet and making the necessary adjustments to live within your means. You can do it! Even though it might mean doing what Debbie and I had to do—that is, sell a nice car that we had no business buying and driving something cheap but reliable for a while. It might mean the disruption and inconvenience of moving. It might mean selling some things. Quitting some things. Unsubscribing from some things. Whatever it takes, it's worth it.

So, that brings us to another question. How can you know how much spending you need to cut? Put another way, How can you determine how deep those cuts in spending need to go? I know a gentleman who not only has the answer to that very important question but is also willing and able to help you live within your means.

I plan to introduce you to him in the next chapter. Read on.

CHAPTER THIRTEEN

HELLO, MR. BUDGET

The fresh, young face looking down at me from the drive-through window at the fast-food restaurant had frozen into a look that was a mixture of bewilderment and panic. And it was all my fault.

This was several years ago when my daughter was still living at home, and we were driving through to grab her something to eat. At the speaker we were informed that our total was $5.57. Now, I only had a twenty-dollar bill and quickly calculated that I was about to be handed a ten, four ones, and forty-three cents in change. I didn't want all those ones and I really didn't want any more pennies rattling around in the change cup. So when we got to the window, I handed the young lady the twenty-dollar bill and said, "Hold on a moment. I think I may have fifty-seven cents." Upon fishing around in the place in my car where I keep my change, I discovered that I did not have exactly fifty-seven cents (no nickel), but I did have sixty-two cents (two quarters, one dime, and two pennies). When I handed the coins over, the poor girl looked down at her hand like I'd just placed a slug-like alien insect in it. Then she looked at the total on the cash register. Then at the twenty-dollar bill. Then back at the coins. Then back at the twenty. She was frozen. Trapped in some sort of endless confusion loop.

I honestly wasn't trying to throw anyone a curve. I had just quickly determined that if I gave her $20.62, my change coming back would be a tidy fifteen dollars and a nickel.

The manager, sensing something was wrong, came over and joined in the problem solving. Once fully apprised of the facts of the case, he got out pen and paper, ciphered for a bit, then looked at me and said uncertainly, "Fifteen dollars and five cents...right?" I nodded and he said, "Whew!" They both looked so relieved.

I don't mean to sound like the old geezer who remembers how much better things were "back in the day," but there really was a time when most people could manage simple money-math problems like making change. I have a friend who created a similar math problem for a cashier at another store. Eventually the cashier just motioned toward the register drawer and told him to just go ahead and take however much he felt he had coming to him.

Please understand—I'm not being unkind. Nor do I mean to pick on young people. I know many people of all ages have challenges with math. In fact, before I teach or preach about budgeting, my sweet wife, Debbie, is faithful to remind me that not everyone can do math in his or her head the way I do. She rightly encourages me to have empathy for those for whom math is more of a challenge. One reason I know many people aren't living within their means is because they struggle with basic math. Frankly, we have a whole society drowning in debt because we apparently can't add, much less comprehend the multiplying power of compound interest.

We love to help people through the stewardship ministry at Gateway Church. It's why we created the department, now overseen by my son, James. When someone who is struggling financially comes in for counseling, one of the first things we do is get a snapshot of their monthly income versus their bills so we can identify the source of their financial problems. Often, the conversation goes something like this:

What is your monthly income?

It's $3,000.

Okay, now let's get a feel for your fixed expenses.

Well, our mortgage is $1,200. We have a $400 car payment and a $360 car payment. Car insurance is $150. Our utilities average around $250. Mobile phone and data charges are $250. Cable TV and internet is $110. The credit card minimum payments are $325 (and rising).

That total already exceeds $3,000, and that's before we've added in childcare, gym memberships, other subscriptions, etc. Then we get into the variable expenses like groceries and eating out. Invariably, our running total exceeds their monthly income by a large margin. And that's well before we've even gotten to periodic, nonmonthly expenses such as medical costs, car repairs, and home maintenance. All this is apart from the conversation we have about the power of putting God first with the tithe.

That math obviously doesn't work. Many times, the reality of the basic arithmetic of their situation comes as a complete surprise for people. Of course, they knew that they consistently ran out of money long before the next pay period. And they were vaguely aware that their credit card balances had been steadily creeping upward. But they didn't know exactly how much more they had obligated themselves to spend than they actually had available.

These are intelligent adults. It's not that they literally can't do the math. It's that they choose not to do it. They don't count what their expenses are and what their income is. Perhaps they don't really *want* to know the truth. Did you know that Jesus warned us against taking this casual, flying-by-the-seat-of-the-pants approach? He did!

In Luke 14, Jesus says,

> For which of you, intending to build a tower, does not sit down first and count the cost, whether he has enough to finish it—lest, after he has laid the foundation, and is not able to finish, all who see it begin to mock him, saying, "This man began to build and was not able to finish"? Or what king, going to make war against another king, does not sit down first and consider whether he is able with ten thousand to meet him who comes against him with twenty thousand? (vv. 28–31)

Jesus uses two illustrations—a builder and a king going to war—to sternly warn us against *not* doing the math! How much house can you afford? (Please note that I didn't ask, How much will the mortgage company loan you? Lenders will almost always loan you more than you have any business borrowing.) What kind of car can you afford to drive? How much can you spend on clothes? How much can you put in savings? How much can you give? You are going to have to do the math if you are going to find reality-based answers to these

> Jesus uses two illustrations—a builder and a king going to war—to sternly warn us against *not* doing the math!

questions and live below your means. Here's the good news: There is already a proven, time-tested tool for doing the kind of math required to get on the path of wise stewardship.

Mr. Budget Is Your Friend

You start with a heart to be a good steward. (If you're still with me here at chapter 13, I'm confident you have one of those.) That leads you to an understanding that you need to do the three things excellent stewards do—that is, commit to spend wisely, save diligently, give generously. In turn, that commitment leads you to set goals in each of those three areas. And achieving those goals requires a specialized tool. There is a highly technical accounting term for that tool. A *budget*.

I know. A budget doesn't sound like a very exotic or ultramodern solution. Here in the twenty-first century, you might be tempted to think surely some new "magic bullet" technology has emerged to keep you from spending more than you earn. I'm sorry, but all the new technology is designed to help you spend more, more easily... not spend less. In contrast, budgets have been around longer than money itself. Think about how an ancient farmer who harvested crops and food in the fall needed to make those provisions last all the way through winter. Running out of food before spring would constitute a life-threatening disaster for a family. Just as an ancient family needed a plan for making sure their food carried them through the winter, your family needs a plan to carry you through each month and into the future.

The only alternative to budgeting is... *not* budgeting. This, sadly, is the option so many believers choose. Which is precisely why most are, at best, living paycheck to paycheck and, more likely, getting farther behind every month. Choosing the "not budgeting" option is the primary reason believers fail in all three facets of wise stewardship—spending, saving, and giving.

In a sense, budgeting is really just spending ALL your money in accordance with your goals. That's right—I said spending "all" your money. One way to think about a budget is as a detailed plan for allocating every cent of your income to the places you've determined in advance and that are in alignment with your goals. When you tithe, you're "spending" the first 10 percent of your income to recognize God's firstness in your heart and His ownership of all. When you put a portion of your paycheck in savings, you're "spending" money to build your future and achieve your goals. That's why my good friend Dave Ramsey says, "A budget is telling your money where to go instead of wondering where it went."

A budget is simply a detailed plan that reflects your values and goals. Most households simply don't have a plan for getting to where they want to go. Think of a good budget as a map for arriving at your goals. Of course, that assumes that you have goals. Where do you want to go? How much money do you want to have in the bank ten years from now? In twenty years? How much would you like to be giving to your church and to causes you're passionate about in ten years? Next year? This year? What kinds of hopes and aspirations has God placed within you?

Whatever your goals are, you won't get there by accident. You won't stumble blindly into that good land. A budget that reflects these values and goals is your road map. In a very real sense, a budget is your best friend and faithful ally in the

> Whatever your goals are, you won't get there by accident.

battle against your own worst habits and impulses. If you let it, a budget can remove the element of emotion from spending decisions. In a previous chapter I pointed out how almost all our choices begin with emotion, and then we ask our intellect to create a rationale for what the gut has already decided it wants. So many foolish spending decisions are rooted in this cycle of impulse, emotion, and rationalization.

Having a budget that everyone in the household takes seriously can interrupt that cycle. It can also remove the emotion from spending decisions in another important way. Often two individuals in a marriage have very different temperaments and approaches to money. One may be naturally frugal and the other a natural spender. One may be cautious and the other impulsive. This often puts one person in the relationship in the no-fun role of being the "bad cop"—the one who is always having to be the wet blanket. A lot of relational tension and resentment can be avoided simply by making the budget the authoritative decision maker. This is doubly important when *both* parties in a marriage are natural "spenders."

That's why around our house we personified our budget early in our relationship. That's right—"Mr. Budget" is a long-standing member of our household. Mr. Budget can be stern, but he's also wise and only has our long-term best interests in mind. When Debbie or I would come across something unplanned or impulsive that one of us wanted to purchase, the other learned to say, "Why, that certainly does look appealing. Let's consult Mr. Budget!" And if the funds for such a purchase weren't allocated, the other of us would say, "Aw, Mr. Budget says, 'No, not at this time.' Gosh, that stinks!" This way neither of us had to be the bad guy in the eyes of the person we love. Mr. Budget also is a powerful ally in saying no to requests and invitations from others that involve spending money.

These could be requests to go on trips, support fundraising events, or go out to fancy restaurants. No one wants to say no to someone they like or have to see at every family event. But Mr. Budget is happy to take the blame for you. "Gosh, Aunt Ida, we'd LOVE to buy a raffle ticket for your 'Save the Endangered Banana Slug' fund-raiser, but we checked our budget and our Discretionary Giving category is already fully committed for the next several months. Maybe next year!"

This is what I mean when I say that having a budget takes the emotional factor out of spending decisions. It allows you to make nonemotional decisions in emotion-inducing circumstances. No one wants to look cheap or poor. How many times have you spent money you didn't really have simply to avoid embarrassment or out of social pressure? Mr. Budget takes the decision out of your hands. You let the budget decide. I tell husbands, when your spouse comes to you and says, "Honey, will you buy this for me?" you can be the supportive good guy and say, "Darling, I would love to buy that for you! Of course, we need to see what Mr. Budget says…Oh no, Mr. Budget says no. I'm so sorry. I would have loved to have seen you in that." Please note that I tell wives that this works both ways. Ladies have just as much power with the budget to say, "Honey, those shiny, new golf clubs look beautiful, and I have no doubt that they will instantly shave eight strokes off your average score, but Mr. Budget says not this year. He's so strict!"

Over the years, I've taught our congregation the powerful secret of bringing Mr. Budget into the family circle. I recall one young mother coming up to me after a service and letting me know that they had fully embraced the "Mr. Budget" concept in their household and that it had really helped them get control of their finances. In fact, she said she had been employing it frequently when one of her three young children asked for something they had no business buying. She mentioned that one of their belt-tightening steps had been to cut way back on eating out at fast-food restaurants. However, they had designated Tuesday nights for going to McDonald's because that's the night you can get a Happy Meal (without a toy) for only one dollar. She told me that on the previous Tuesday night, she heard her daughter's little voice from the back seat of the minivan say, "Mom, can I get a toy with my Happy Meal tonight?" Her reply was, "Oh, honey, we've talked about this. I'd love to do that for you, but Mr. Budget says no on that." There was a moment of thoughtful silence in the vehicle; then she heard the same voice coldly say, "Mom, I want Mr. Budget to die."

I laughed especially hard when I heard that, because I knew exactly how that girl felt! I felt that way frequently back when Debbie and I were taking our first steps toward getting our finances in order and practicing wise stewardship. But here's what I discovered. Mr. Budget really is a good guy. After you've consistently followed his counsel for a while—especially once you begin to see the blessing that invariably results from practicing good stewardship— you'll begin to hear Mr. Budget say yes much more often!

> You will never fulfill the wonderful destiny God has envisioned for your life if you cannot manage your finances. And it begins with a budget.

I'm being humorous, but there is a very serious truth at the root of all this. We get into trouble when we wait until the heat of the moment to decide what our spending priorities are. A budget isn't an opinion. A line item on your spending plan isn't a feeling. It's objective, detached, and factual. And if both parties in a marriage will commit to taking it seriously, it will provide a protective layer of accountability and consistency that will discipline your spending so it stays in line with your goals.

A budget is an indispensable part of wise stewardship because it delivers so many benefits. A budget:

- helps you see things more clearly and objectively;
- makes you examine and clarify your values and priorities;
- provides a basis of discussion and agreement;
- helps you live within your means;
- helps you live free from the bondage of debt; and
- builds character and discipline in your life.

Frankly, you will never fulfill the wonderful destiny God has envisioned for your life if you cannot manage your finances. And it begins with a budget. Of course, this leads to the matter of *how* to go about creating one.

From Envelopes to Apps

Many people don't have a budget simply because they don't know how to build one. The good news is that it's never been easier. Today, a huge array of tools, guides, and helps exist to guide you through the process. Dave Ramsey has a great one called Every Dollar available at his website (daveramsey.com). In addition to personal finance programs like Quicken, there are many other apps out there like Mint or YNAB (which stands for You Need a Budget). We also have free budgeting forms on our church's stewardship website (stewardship.gatewaypeople.com). Some of these tools are online and can be accessed digitally. Most of these will take you through some of the key steps to building and sticking to a budget. These steps should include the following:

- **Courageously Evaluate Your Current Situation**

When you're in a mess, it's tempting to just stick your head in the sand. I've known of people who got behind on their bills and just stopped opening the envelopes when the past-due notices started showing up in the mail. Some irrational part of their brain told them that if they didn't open the bills and see the amount due, the obligation somehow didn't really exist. In a similar way, some people just don't really want a clear picture of where they stand. Of course, that kind of denial is a prescription for disaster. What you don't know can and will hurt you.

Anyone who has gone through a twelve-step program to overcome alcoholism or addiction will tell you that step four is to undertake "a fearless and searching moral inventory." Breaking your addiction to bad financial management requires a comparable step. As I noted in chapter 11 in my discussion on goal setting, you have to begin your journey by knowing precisely where you are. If your situation is messy, that may require asking God for the courage to face the whole ugly truth. This means identifying not only every debt but every asset, too. Assets can be liquidated or sold to pay debts. Start with a clear and comprehensive picture of what you have and what you owe.

- **Review Your Income and Spending**

Most people know how much they make. The majority of households get paid the same amount once or twice each month. This makes planning on the income side relatively easy. Of course, that's not true for everyone. People who work in commissioned sales or for tips experience a lot of fluctuations in their income. Other people have seasonal peaks and valleys in their income. For these folks, budget planning is a bit more challenging but not impossible.

One approach is to take your average income over the last twelve months, then base your budget on 80 to 85 percent of that amount. That way a month or two of lower-than-average income won't wreck your budget. Also, if you're building your budget on a variable income stream, it's important to go extra heavy in the emergency savings category (which we'll discuss in a moment). Just as Joseph wisely led the Egyptians to do in Genesis 41, you'll be laying up extra during the "fat" months to carry you through the "lean" months.

Once you have a firm grip on your income, it's time to take the more complex (and potentially painful) step of reviewing your expenses. It's important to account for every penny you are spending each month, including any cash you're spending if you or your spouse tend to withdraw cash from ATMs and spend it on miscellaneous expenses. It's also vital to account for all expenses that tend to end up on your credit cards. Many households have numerous subscriptions that are automatically charged to a card each and every month.

As you are reviewing all your expenses, it's helpful to sort them into several broad categories. First, almost all spending can be viewed as either mandatory or discretionary. Mandatory expenses are those that must be paid each month. For example, rent or mortgage payments, car payments, and insurance premiums must be paid on time. If you stop paying them, there are going to be big problems. Discretionary spending is that which you have a measure of control over. Your grocery spending, entertainment expenses, dining out, and many other types of spending fall under this category.

Another way to view expenses is as either fixed or variable. Some mandatory expenses are fixed—meaning the amount is the same every month. Others, such as utility bills and mobile phone charges (depending upon data usage), vary from month to month.

Finally, expenses can and should be classified as either monthly or periodic. Some bills like insurance premiums and homeowners' association dues may come due only once or twice per year. And expenses such as car repairs, home repairs, or medical expenses can occur at any time unexpectedly. All of these varying types of expenses should be accounted for in your budget.

Again, there are a number of great online tools and services out there to help you through this process of categorization. Many of these are free because they are driven by advertisements. (Just don't be swayed by the ads!)

Once you have a clear handle on your debts, assets, income, and current spending—this represents where you currently are—you're ready to start crafting your plan for getting to a better place.

- **Identify Values and Goals**

Building a budget requires making choices. Sometimes, these choices are difficult. That's why it is vital to establish what's most important to you *before* you start deciding where you're going to cut. As we saw in chapter 5, good stewards put first things first. But

> Building a budget requires making choices.

to do that you have to know what your "first things" are.

In his time management book, *First Things First*, Stephen Covey relates a powerful illustration of this principle.[1] He describes a group of ambitious MBA students assembled for a seminar on time management. In the middle of his talk, the instructor said, "Okay, time for a quiz," and produced a big, widemouthed glass jar, setting it on a table in front of him. Then he brought out about a dozen fist-sized rocks. One by one he carefully placed them into the jar until it was filled to the top and no more rocks would fit inside. Then he asked the class, "Is this jar full?" Every head in the class nodded. In response he said, "Really?" He then reached under the table and pulled out a bucket of pea-sized gravel. Then he dumped some gravel into the jar and shook it, causing pieces of gravel to work themselves down into the spaces between the larger rocks.

Then he smiled and asked the group once more, "Now is the jar full?" By this time the class was wary. "Probably not," one of them answered. "Good!" he replied. And he reached under the table and brought out a bucket of sand and proceeded to dump it in. The sand easily settled into all the spaces left between the rocks and the gravel. Once more he asked the question, "Is this jar full?" The class was silent. Smiling, the teacher took a pitcher of water and poured it in until the jar was filled to the brim. Then he looked up at the class and asked, "Can anyone tell me what the point of this illustration is?"

One eager beaver raised his hand and ventured, "The point is no matter how full you think your schedule is, you can always fit some more things into it!"

"No," the speaker replied, "that's not the point. The truth this illustration teaches us is: If you don't put the big rocks in first, you'll never get them in at all." Put another way, if you don't schedule and prioritize the most important things you need to accomplish in your day, you'll never fit them in. In other words, first things first.

What is true of your time and schedule is also true of your money and budget. You have to put "the big rocks" in first, or you will never get them in at all! I urge you in the strongest possible terms, for your sake and the sake of your family, make honoring God with your "firstfruits" a priority. If you love God, are grateful to Him for saving and adopting you to be His own, and want His ongoing blessing on your life, He must be the first of your "first things." That means budgeting your tithe first.

• **Plan to Save**

Another "big rock" should be putting as much money as possible in savings each month. I've heard these two priorities summarized as, "Pay God; then pay yourself; then pay everyone else." Of course, if you're also trying to get out of debt, the amounts you put into savings may be smaller in the beginning, but you at least will want to start building up an emergency fund to cover unexpected expenses such as repairs and medical costs. But ultimately the objective in learning to live well below your means is to be able to save a significant portion of your income each month.

Someone once asked me if I believed it was appropriate for a Christian to have a savings account. I was a little surprised by the question. Apparently, some people have been taught that Jesus' comment in Matthew 6 about laying up treasure in heaven as opposed to on earth means that it's wrong for believers to have savings accounts. To emphasize a point, my answer was, "No, I don't think Christians should have *a* savings account. I think they should have five of them!"

It's true. Now, I don't think you literally need five separate accounts with distinct account numbers. But I do think you need to be accumulating money in at least one savings account for five distinct purposes, with the dollars for each purpose earmarked and tracked. What are these five purposes? I've already mentioned the first of them.

1. Emergencies: You need to be able to handle a significant car or home repair or medical bill without it wrecking your entire financial plan. If you're just starting out in your career or in marriage, you may only have an emergency fund of $1,000. As you continue on in life, the appropriate amount might grow to $5,000; $10,000; or more. Whatever your situation or season of life, there is some specific amount that you should prayerfully decide you will never allow your savings account to get below. Many advisors suggest building up an emergency fund in savings equal to about three to six months of living expenses. This is your buffer for emergencies.

2. Needs: Clothes and shoes wear out. Kids require braces. And other large expenses come along from time to time. Everything from education expenses for kids to replacing cars. These are needs rather than wants, but you'll want to avoid using debt to pay for these things. For example, it's best to pay cash for your cars because they depreciate so rapidly. At the very minimum, you'll want to make a very large down payment on a vehicle so that you never owe more than it's worth. But it is ideal to avoid financing car purchases altogether. That requires saving for your next car while the one you're currently driving is still perfectly good.

3. Wants: There is nothing wrong with wanting a new set of golf clubs or a new purse or a family vacation. However, to use debt to finance these things is foolish and counterproductive to your stewardship goals. If you want something, save for it and pay cash. It's by far the most gratifying and satisfying way to fulfill these desires. Part of your regular saving discipline should be to set money aside for things you desire.

As I pointed out in Chapter 6, you'll enjoy them much more if you delay gratification, wait, and ultimately pay cash.

4. The future: We all grow older. Retirement is optional, but slowing down a bit as you age isn't. You'll want to save for your twilight years and in order to leave something for the next generation to build upon.

5. Giving: This may be the most important reason of all to save, yet most people never even think about it. I've already addressed the joy of giving. Responding to a prompting from the Spirit of God to bless someone else or fund something God wants to accomplish is one of the most thrilling things you can experience this side of heaven. Have you ever given an extravagant gift to God? (The principle of the widow's mite teaches us that what constitutes "extravagant" is purely a function of how much you have.) In my previous book, *The Blessed Life*, I share several stories of times Debbie and I emptied one or more of our savings accounts in order to participate in something God was doing. We've never once regretted doing so. On the contrary, the joy and blessing we experienced as a result each time were extraordinary.

You can experience that, too, but only if you begin budgeting for it. If you've never felt the Spirit of God nudging you to give in this way, perhaps that is because you've not had it to give. Why would God ask you to do something you haven't put your-

> Start a savings fund expressly for the purpose of giving over and above the tithe and watch what happens!

self in a position to do? Start a savings fund expressly for the purpose of giving over and above the tithe and watch what happens!

Obviously, having a savings account is biblical and appropriate for God's people! In God's wisdom book, Proverbs, we learn that only foolish people don't anticipate future needs and save for them. ("Consider the ant!"—Proverbs 6:6) And don't forget His wonderful promises for those who put Him first:

Honor the LORD with your possessions,
and with the firstfruits of all your increase;
so your barns will be filled with plenty,
and your vats will overflow with new wine. (Proverbs 3:9–10)

Metaphorically, your "barns" are the places you store for the future. However, as your savings begins to grow, it's vital to keep two of the most basic truths of stewardship in mind.

First, never forget that it all belongs to God. Hold everything material, including your savings accounts, with an open hand. You're a steward, not an owner. This is the mind-set that is vital when the Spirit of God prompts you to give an extravagant gift for His kingdom. Second, never forget that God, not money, is your sole source of security and significance. Once your savings begins to grow, it's tempting to start thinking of your bank balance as the source of your security. That's the spirit of Mammon talking. Don't fall for it.

After you've placed all the "big rocks" in your budget, then you're ready to move on to the rest of your expenses. You'll add in everything that you categorized as a "mandatory" expense—including your fixed, variable, and periodic bills. For the variable expenses, take a twelve-month average.

Where this process gets serious is when you move on to the discretionary spending. Here is where you find out how serious you really are about living within your means and becoming a wise steward. As you begin, lay everything on the altar and keep your goals in view. Be brutally honest with yourself. Can you really afford to be driving the cars you currently have in your driveway? You may really feel that your gym membership, ultrafast internet, multitiered cable package, salon treatments, and date nights at five-star restaurants are "essentials." But are they really? Or should they be sacrificed for a season so you can step into a life of long-term peace and power?

Cut, cancel, hack, slice, trim, and shave until you have an expense budget that represents less than your income. Depending upon your circumstances, doing this will range somewhere between "quite painful" and "excruciating." But it's worth it. You're saying no to some things in the short term in order to say a big YES to something far more valuable. Keep your eyes on the prize of your goals.

> God will respond to your sincere steps of obedience with His power and provision.

Let me also reiterate that God will respond to your sincere steps of obedience with His power and provision. Your firm commitment to become a faithful steward will be met with heavenly help!

Following Your Budget

Once you've created your budget road map, the real test comes as you begin to follow it, day after day, week after week, pay period by pay period. The most brilliantly crafted budget in the world—one that perfectly reflects both your realities and your goals—is utterly useless if you're not going to honor it by following through. Give Mr. Budget the respect he deserves! He's there to help you!

Not too many years ago, most spending was done with either cash or check. Today both seem to be on the endangered species list. Debit cards replaced checks a while ago, and now digital mobile payment systems embedded in your smartphone are rapidly making debit cards obsolete.

Back in the cash-and-check days, tracking your expenses by category required diligently saving your receipts for every single expenditure large and small, then regularly entering them into some record-keeping system by category. Personal finance software programs like Quicken came along and made this kind of record keeping quite a bit easier. But you still had to diligently enter every transaction in and tag it to the proper spending category.

In that previous era, many diligent people on a budget employed an "envelope system" to help them manage their discretionary spending. The month's budgeted allotment for certain categories of spending such as groceries, eating out, entertainment, and clothing was placed in its respective envelope. Money for each category was spent throughout the month, and when the allotment was gone, it was gone. It was a clear and powerful way to create spending discipline in areas that have the tendency to drift out of control as we lose track of them. That's still a very sound approach if you want to utilize it.

As I noted previously, this emerging era of paperless, electronic transactions has made it easier than ever to spend money.

One positive aspect, however, is that it has also made it easier than ever to track and monitor your spending. Again, numerous online tools are available that you can link to your bank accounts and use to keep a handle on your finances in real time. For example, the new versions of Quicken automatically pull all your expenses from your bank account and card accounts and classify them for you based off how you normally classify each expense and deposit.

Again, my purpose here is not to tell you everything you need to know and do in order to establish and follow a budget. Other resources can do that for you. My goal is to motivate you to get started! Decide today to start living within your means. And get started by committing to a lifestyle of budgeting. Cultivating the discipline of budgeting helps make you a person God can entrust with more.

> Decide today to start living within your means.

Increase will destroy bad stewards. But God can and will channel more resources into the hands of people who spend, save, and give in accordance with what He values. Now let's explore some principles and practices concerning one of the most important topics of our day. Let's learn how to think about debt.

CHAPTER FOURTEEN

TO DEBT, OR NOT TO DEBT

I may be about to shock you. Especially since you've already read chapter 8, in which I compared financing things you can't afford to running a Ponzi scheme on yourself and stealing from your own future. I hope you're sitting down.

I'm not against *all* debt in *all* circumstances. I don't think borrowing is uniformly, categorically, universally evil. I don't believe the Bible teaches that good stewards never, ever borrow. Nor do I think carrying a credit card is a mortal sin. As I've already mentioned, I carry a credit card or two. I've even taught my adult children to carry and responsibly use credit cards. They, with my blessing and encouragement, have home mortgages. In other words, I'm not an absolutist on the subject of debt.

I know that sets me apart from most leading money management advisors out there today—especially those to whom many Christians look for guidance. These tend to have a view of debt and borrowing that can be summarized this way:

"No!"

I'm joking. But it's true that most strongly advise people to cut up their credit cards, eliminate all debt, and never borrow again. I certainly understand why they take that position. They spend all their time trying to help people who have allowed debt to nearly ruin their lives and who are going to have to go through years of extraordinary, disciplined effort to dig out of the hole they're in. I get it.

Although I respect and admire these experts and point people to their resources all the time, I'd like to offer a slightly different viewpoint. In the process I'll lay out a balanced biblical view of debt, highlight its dangers and pitfalls, and offer you some guidelines and questions to ask yourself when you're contemplating borrowing money.

Let's get started.

Defining Debt

Every once in a while, someone living in Turkey, Iraq, or Iran—the modern nations that now constitute the area known in ancient times as Mesopotamia—will stick a shovel in the ground and turn up a hollow little pillow-shaped piece of clay with something rattling around inside.

Archaeologists familiar with that part of the world know that these little containers are thousands of years old, served as an ancient type of envelope, and that the hard, little pieces of clay rattling around inside are "tokens" that represent the details of a debt. These tokens of various shapes and sizes represent specific quantities of grain or oil. If one person wanted to sell another person some grain or oil on credit, they would create one of these to record the details of the transaction so both could be reminded of what was owed. These little clay pods and tokens have been found all over that part of the world and predate the invention of writing by thousands of years.

Here is the significance of these debt pods. They tell us that long before there was either writing or money, there was borrowing and lending. As long as people have been living in communities or in proximity to one another, they have been writing each other IOUs. Imagine two ancient Mesopotamian farmers who live near one another. "Bob" lives in the valley and grows barley, which ripens in the spring. "Tom" lives up on the side of the mountain and tends olive trees, which ripen in late summer or early fall. Bob and Tom would like to trade for each other's produce, but money doesn't exist. There is no medium of exchange to facilitate that transaction. So one spring, Tom approaches Bob with an idea. "You give me several bushel baskets of your barley now, and I'll give you the equivalent value in olive oil when my trees ripen in a few months." This is appealing to Bob as he has long admired the quality of Tom's olive oil, and he needs oil to make bread. So they come to an agreement. Tom makes some little clay tokens that represent how many jugs of olive oil he owes Bob, seals them into a pouch or pod made of wet clay, and impresses some marks into the clay that serve as the equivalent of his unique signature. Then he fires that clay until it's hardened like a piece of pottery and hands it over to Bob as his personal IOU. That way there is no misunderstanding down the line about what was agreed upon. It's a brilliant little system because Bob can't cheat by adding extra tokens without breaking the clay pod open, and Tom can't "misremember" how much he promised to pay.

As I said, archaeologists have found thousands of these little IOUs buried throughout the region of ancient Mesopotamia dating back to the dawn of civilization. Debt was also clearly a fact of economic life in early biblical times as well, so much so that God, through Moses, gave the Israelites highly specific instructions about lending—including who they could and could not charge interest, what could and should not be held as security for a loan, as well as when and how debts must be forgiven. (For example, see Exod. 22:25–27, Lev. 25:36–37, and Deut. 23:20–22.) The Bible's sternest warnings about loaning money center on the charging of interest (usury). Then, as now, it is the way interest charges compound over time that makes debt so potentially dangerous for the borrower and so lucrative for the lender.

However, at the most basic level, debt is simply owing something to someone else. Of course, in our day what is owed is, more often than not, money. This brings us to the question of whether it is ever appropriate or prudent for a believer to borrow money. To find an answer, we should examine what the Bible says about debt. Doing so yields a more complicated answer than you might expect.

Debt in the Bible

In the book of Leviticus, God encourages His people to loan money or food (without interest) to fellow Israelites who are struggling, in order to help them get back on their feet (Lev. 25:35–37). There is a much longer parallel passage in Deuteronomy in which God, through Moses, provides scriptural guidelines for lending money, especially to the poor and struggling:

> For the LORD your God will bless you just as He promised you; you shall lend to many nations, but you shall not borrow; you shall reign over many nations, but they shall not reign over you.

If there is among you a poor man of your brethren, within any of the gates in your land which the LORD your God is giving you, you shall not harden your heart nor shut your hand from your poor brother, but you shall open your hand wide to him and willingly lend him sufficient for his need, whatever he needs. (Deuteronomy 15:6–8)

There are several things I want to point out about this passage because it is frequently quoted as a proof text that God's people should never borrow.

First of all, if borrowing money is always and only a curse upon the person who borrows, why would a loving God, who clearly cares about the poor, command His people to lend to them? Yes, He's talking about interest-free loans, but they're still loans. God is not punishing the poor here. He's encouraging His people to help them in a way that does not promote dependency or incentivize idleness—the twin hazards of welfare.

The first part of that passage is frequently cited as a prohibition against Christians ever borrowing money: "For the LORD your God will bless you just as He promised you; you shall lend to many nations, but you shall not borrow."

Many people have misunderstood that last phrase. That's a prophecy, not a command. He's not forbidding them to borrow. He's declaring that they will be so blessed they won't need to. When you have an abundance, you don't have to borrow. You can lend instead. This is what God predicts for His people if they will keep His covenant statutes. Wealthy nations lend to poorer nations. God is saying, "Stick with me and you'll be a wealthy nation." He's clearly not saying borrowing is evil, because immediately following this we see a command to lend to their fellow Israelites who are having a hard time.

By the way, you may recall me telling you about my dad and his little black ledger book in the opening pages of this book. In the light of this passage, you can now appreciate that he was and is a living embodiment of this biblical truth. He is a good steward, so God has blessed him. This gives him an abundance with which he helps his struggling brothers and sisters in Christ by offering them low- to no-interest loans to help them get on their feet.

Furthermore, God is speaking to the Israelites more as a nation here, than as individuals. What God is saying is that He wants to make a shining example of them as a collective people. In other words, "I want to show the world what it looks like when My blessing rests upon an entire people instead of just a few individuals." It would be like God saying to the church it is my privilege to pastor, "I am going to prove that I am with you by blessing you so much you will never have to borrow as a church. But as individual members, you will still need to help each other out individually from time to time." It doesn't mean that every single church member will always be debt-free.

That passage begins with the promise of God's blessing. It's that blessing that puts them into a position to have such an abundance that they are lenders rather than borrowers—people who are able to help others rather than needing help. That is precisely why I've written this book on being a wise steward. Wise stewards get blessed, and blessed people can be lenders, sharers, and generous givers.

> Wise stewards get blessed, and blessed people can be lenders, sharers, and generous givers.

Commendable, Not Commandable

This isn't to suggest that I think incurring debt is a good thing. That should be clear based on everything I've communicated up to this point. Or that there aren't inherent hazards in borrowing, especially since borrowing in our day involves interest charges. Nevertheless, there are times, circumstances, and contexts in which the believer may utilize—with caution and prudence—the tool of debt. One way I like to encapsulate this balanced truth is to say that I view being debt-free as "commendable, not commandable."

In other words, it's a very desirable thing to be completely free from debt, but it should not be viewed as a commandment from God. We're not violating some sacred moral principle if we responsibly, prudently use debt for something like a home mortgage. It's not God's best, but it doesn't disqualify you for blessing, either.

Those who would make getting and staying debt-free a *command* rather than merely an ideal cite Romans 13:8 to bolster their case. That verse reads, "Owe no one anything except to love one another, for he who loves another has fulfilled the law." They would say, "See there! The Bible says not to owe anybody anything." There are two problems with that interpretation. The first is that the context of this verse is Paul talking about our relationship to the law of Moses under the New Covenant. The verses that follow talk about commandments against lying, stealing, murdering, and so forth. All these sins were viewed as incurring an obligation, or debt, to your neighbor. This sense of wronging someone being a type of *debt* is reflected in the language of the King James Version of the Lord's Prayer: "Forgive us our debts, as we forgive our debtors" (Matt. 6:12). Echoing what Jesus told some experts in the law one day, Paul is saying loving your neighbor fulfills all your obligations to them and to the law. In other words, don't worry about keeping each individual Old Covenant commandment, law, and regulation. Just love your neighbor and you'll naturally fulfill the spirit of them all.

The second problem with interpreting Romans 13:8 as a prohibition against debt is that it would be literally impossible to obey in a literal way. We all occasionally *owe* other people, if only briefly. For example, if you sit down at a restaurant and order a meal, you owe the restaurant the total cost of your food up until the time you pay the bill. For however long you're sitting there enjoying your food, you're indebted to the restaurant. Employers owe their employees their accrued wages for several days, then ultimately settle up on payday. You accumulate a debt to the electric company throughout the month and then pay the bill before the due date the company has specified. I know I'm splitting hairs here, but it's important to acknowledge the reality that we all use debt on pretty much a daily basis. The only question is, Do we use it and manage it responsibly or irresponsibly?

Sadly, for many believers, the answer to that question is no. Which brings us to another point at which I respectfully differ somewhat with the leading personal finance advisors—the question of credit cards.

The Credit Card Question

If the leading advisors are generally against debt, they're really, really against credit cards. And I understand why. It's extraordinarily easy to get yourself into trouble with credit card debt. And millions of Americans have done just that. An August 2017 report published online on the financial site MarketWatch.com reported that Americans had just set a dubious new record:

American consumers just hit a scary milestone. They now collectively have the most outstanding revolving debt—often summarized as credit card debt—in U.S. history, according to a report Monday released by the Federal Reserve. Americans had $1.021 trillion in outstanding revolving credit in June 2017.[1]

That's right. That's more than a trillion with a *t* in credit card debt. And that's on top of mortgage loans, car loans, and student loans. At least with mortgage and auto loan debt, there is something of value securing the loan (which is why the interest rates tend to be lower). Credit card debt is utterly unsecured. As a result, the interest rates most people end up paying are ridiculously high, especially if they've ever been late on even a single payment or gone one dollar over their credit limit. In these cases, the rates skyrocket to levels that make it very difficult for people to ever extricate themselves from the mess.

Being in the credit card business is extraordinarily lucrative, precisely because most people today have no financial discipline or impulse control. There are fortunes to be made in usury—which is loaning money at exorbitant interest rates. This is why God forbade His people from loaning money at interest to their fellow Israelites. It's also why your mailbox is full of credit card offers every day. These companies are not your friend. They do not have your best interests at heart. And they make stealing from your own future to satisfy a craving or to get out of a short-term jam extremely tempting.

Like the young wife whose story I shared in chapter 8, credit cards make it possible to feed an addiction to spending and dig yourself into a hole that can seem impossible to climb out of.

Given all that, I can certainly understand why some just advise people to avoid credit cards altogether. You certainly can't abuse one if you don't have one. However, I liken that to avoiding owning a car simply because so many other people are poor drivers and large numbers of people get hurt on the highways each year. There are a lot of benefits that come from being a responsible, prudent car driver. But if you're incapable of driving without endangering yourself and others, then by all means, don't own a car.

I've already mentioned in a previous chapter that I carry a credit card or two and pay the balances off in full every month. This is the only prudent way I would ever recommend managing a credit card. I do this primarily for points and for convenience when traveling. Likewise, I've raised my children to be responsible with money and to be good stewards. So, I've had no concerns about them carrying a credit card or two, either. I've encouraged them to follow my example and never carry a balance. Paying interest on unsecured debt is poor stewardship. You're better off waiting and saving up.

Please understand that I'm not advising you to run out and apply for a credit card if you don't have one. I'm simply saying that for individuals who are good stewards and disciplined money managers, credit cards can be a beneficial tool. And you're not sinning against God or violating an eternal moral principle by carrying one. (Unless, of course, the Spirit of God directs you otherwise. Pray about all decisions and follow His peace!)

Let's move on to some things I would encourage you to consider before taking on any kind of debt.

Making Wise Debt Decisions

Having established that it's permissible under *some* circumstances to carry *certain kinds* of debt for limited seasons of time, it's vital to understand the larger objective. Most of God's people are carrying way,

> Eliminating all debt from your life is commendable (even if it isn't commandable).

way too much debt. If you've been an unwise steward up to this point in your life, you're probably in that boat, and one of your top objectives—second only to putting God first in your finances—must be attacking your debt. Becoming debt-free is a wonderful, powerful goal. As I said, eliminating all debt from your life is commendable (even if it isn't commandable).

If you're carrying credit card debt, student loans, or making car payments on cars you really can't afford to be driving, one of your top priorities in your new lifestyle of wise stewardship is going after that debt as aggressively as possible. Attack the balances with the highest interest rates first. Ordinarily the answer to debt is not "more debt." However, in certain cases where ruthless credit card companies have jumped interest rates to the obscenely high upper limits, it might make sense to refinance these debts at a lower rate. Here's a warning, though. People who have not also fully committed to a lifestyle of wise stewardship often find themselves running their card balances back up again. As a result, they end up worse off than before! If you're not sure you can refrain from abusing your credit cards, close the accounts.

Do whatever is necessary for as long as necessary to get out from under the burden of debt and then continue that lifestyle of financial wisdom by saving and paying as you go. Spend wisely. Save judiciously. Give generously. That's a life of freedom. It's a life of impact. It's a wonderful, peaceful, purpose-filled life.

Once you're living that life, you can approach ongoing decisions about entering into debt wisely and prudently. Debt is a tool that can, under certain well-defined circumstances, make sense. I

recommend approaching debt like
it's a big dog you've never met before.
You don't know if it will be friendly
or vicious, so it's best to approach
with great caution and do your due

> Approach debt like
> it's a big dog you've
> never met before.

diligence before you reach out to pat it on the head. Here are a few
keys to processing a decision about borrowing.

First, see if there is another way. Often people default to borrowing due simply to a lack of imagination or information. Sometimes
there is another avenue that hasn't been considered. Borrowing
should always be an option of last resort.

Second, if you are considering borrowing, formulate an escape
plan. Before you sign on the dotted line, know in advance how you
would pay the obligation off in full quickly if you absolutely had
to. This might involve tapping a savings or investment account
that you ordinarily consider to be off-limits but could access in an
emergency. For example, I previously shared the testimony of Steve
Dulin, who had an investment account earning 8 percent interest
that he used to pay off a loan that had a rate of less than 3 percent.
He made that decision because the Lord specifically instructed him
to do so. Obeying what you believe God is telling you to do always
trumps everything else. In similar circumstances, you might prayerfully consider leaving a high-returning investment account in place
while entering into a low interest rate loan. That account, however,
would represent your emergency escape path. You would borrow
knowing that if necessary, you could pay off the loan in full.

When our youngest, Elaine, was about to head off to college out
of state, we knew she was going to be spending a lot of time on
the highway driving back and forth. We wanted her to have a safe,
reliable car if she was going to be living that far away from home.

After praying about the decision and getting a green light from the Lord, I visited a friend who owned a Toyota dealership. Now, as I mentioned, I'm a big advocate of paying cash for cars because they depreciate so rapidly, and I was prepared to pay cash for Elaine's car. That was the plan. I'm also an advocate of buying used cars rather than new ones. In most cases, it makes much more sense to purchase a two- or three-year-old vehicle that has already taken the initial big hit of depreciation.

In this case, however, we were being offered an exceptionally good deal on a new economy car. I knew this because I'd done my homework in advance and knew what models I was interested in and the average negotiated price they were selling for in my area. So this became a rare case in which I was comfortable buying a new vehicle. I was still planning to pay cash, however. Then I was told that 0 percent financing was available. This presented me with an interesting decision. The money to purchase the vehicle was sitting in a bank account earning a little interest. Not much, but a little. Toyota was willing to provide an interest-free loan. (Moses would have approved!) Plus, some additional perks were thrown in if I took the financing option. I prayed about it briefly and felt a peace about leaving my money in the bank and using that fund to make the payments over time. I had my "exit strategy" in place should I feel the need to eliminate the debt quickly. The car turned out to be a great blessing to my daughter—reliable, efficient, and held its resale value well as we took great care of it.

That leads me to my third recommendation for evaluating a decision about borrowing. That is, "Do the math." (Yes, I said the *m* word again!) In fact, follow your eighth-grade math teacher's advice and do the math, then double-check your work. Then have your mom check it again.

Examine the decision and the terms of it from every angle. Know exactly where you are, where you are going, and how this decision will get you there. Making wise financial decisions often boils down to getting answers to three basic questions. First and foremost, Would doing this violate any biblical principles? Second, Is this mathematically sound? In other words, Have I actually calculated the costs over time and compared the answer to other avenues? Finally, you must ask, Do I have peace in my spirit about this?

Two anecdotes come to mind that illustrate the importance of diligently doing the math in advance.

Before my son James came to work at Gateway Church and ultimately became the head of our stewardship department, he held jobs in a couple of different industries. Right out of college, he worked for a time as a project manager for a fast-growing Dallas home builder. His duties included looking in daily on construction projects scattered all over the Dallas–Fort Worth Metroplex, so he was routinely putting more than one thousand miles per week on his car. That vehicle was very long in the tooth, had high miles on it, and had been owned, free and clear, for some time. Given the age and mileage on the car, it soon became evident that the vehicle simply wasn't up to the task.

James has always been a frugal, prudent guy, so he began tracking what he was spending on repairs and what he was projected to spend in the coming months. The cost was already painfully high, and his mechanic told him he had a new engine in his near future, as well. He projected he needed to be budgeting close to $1,000 per month just to keep that current car on the road. Viewing his problem through the lens of good stewardship, it became painfully apparent that he needed to find a way to replace that car. Ideally, he would pay cash for one, but being fresh out of college, his savings account wasn't adequate—although he had been saving diligently since getting that job.

After praying about it, James moved forward on purchasing the best used car he could afford. He set about prayerfully looking for the best deal he could find. My savvy and successful business owner and friend Steve Dulin teaches that you don't make your money when you *sell*; you actually make it when you *buy*. By that he means that the key to making a profit when you buy and sell things—whether they are houses, cars, stocks, or businesses—is to buy them well. In other words, the key is getting a great deal.

James also knew how much money he had saved up for a down payment. Since he was going to have to finance the purchase, he knew it was important to pay down a big enough percentage of the car's value so it would always be worth more than he owed. This was his "escape strategy." He wanted to be sure that if he absolutely had to liquidate the debt, he could comfortably sell the car for more than he owed at any time.

He also factored in the tax implications. This, too, is a part of "doing the math." Because all that driving was an unreimbursed work expense, he knew he would be able to take a significant deduction on his expenses and depreciation on his tax return. Ultimately, he found a great deal on a reliable car he could afford. It wasn't flashy. It wasn't going to impress anybody. But it got him where he was going safely and dependably. As he drove it, he kept a careful record of his expenses. After tax savings, the math revealed that he was spending less money per mile driving this better car than he most likely would have done keeping and repairing the old one.

He enjoyed the car and paid more than the minimum payment each month, meaning that he retired the debt several months early. Yes, he would have preferred to pay cash for that car and, in the years since, has done so with another car. But he has provided us a great example of how to approach borrowing when it's necessary and prudent.

I want to contrast his story with another one we encountered at Gateway Church's stewardship ministry. It serves as an important example of (almost) not doing the math.

We had a single mother on a very tight budget come to us looking for counsel on buying a vehicle. I'm so glad she did! She was about to purchase an older, used SUV that she had just test-driven at a local used car lot whose advertising shouted, "Bad credit? No credit? No problem! We'll get you financed!" She had been pressured to sign a financing agreement right there on the spot, but she wisely refused. She insisted on taking the details of the deal and financing to my son James in our stewardship ministry.

James sat down with this sweet lady to find out if this obligation she was about to make made sound financial sense. That began with doing the math, so he got out a pen and legal pad to get the facts. After hearing a description of the SUV, he asked about the agreed-upon purchase price. She said the price was $11,000, and she was planning on putting $2,000 down. The dealership was going to provide financing for the balance of $9,000. And the payment? She said it would be $385 per month. James felt like this sounded pretty high for a $9,000 note unless the term of the loan was fairly short. "Is this a three-year loan?" he asked. She answered, "No, the term is four years."

James was surprised and went to work on his calculator. Forty-eight payments of $385 totaled $18,480 in payments. Add in the $2,000 down payment and James determined that she was being pressured into paying more than $20,000 total for an $11,000 purchase. But it was actually worse than that. James then checked several sources for the true value of the SUV. He discovered that a fair dealer price of that vehicle based on the mileage, options, and condition was closer to $9,000.

Given the real value of the vehicle she was considering buying, she would have been upside down from day one—in other words, owing more than she could sell it for. And at that true value, the effective simple interest rate they were charging her on the loan was roughly 127 percent!

Once James went over these numbers with her, it was abundantly clear that she needed to walk away. He helped steer her toward a trustworthy seller and lender, and she was able to acquire a vehicle in a prudent way.

My point is good stewardship requires good math—especially when considering acquiring debt. Like the prudent king and builder in Jesus' parable, we have to count the cost, in both the short and long term.

In addition to looking outward at the details and realities of the transaction and financing, it's vital to also look inward. Check your heart and examine your motives with brutal honesty. Have you been seduced by greed or a desire to impress others? Or is this legitimately justifiable? Keep in mind our very human tendency to rationalize what we desire.

> Check your heart and examine your motives with brutal honesty.

After you've checked your heart, check with God. Pray. Make sure that you allowed God to speak to you through the voice of His Spirit and through His Word. Don't act until you have peace to move forward. Note that I said *peace*, not excitement. Sometimes you can be misguided by excitement for the new thing you are about to get.

A Time to Borrow, and a Time to Eliminate Debt

I want to end this chapter with a praise report that just happened at Gateway Church as I was writing this book. Back in 2009, we knew we needed a much larger sanctuary. We had experienced remarkable growth as a church for several years. The congregation gave very generously, but we still had to borrow several million dollars to complete the project. We diligently did the math and realized that our payment would be less than 5 percent of our income yet would allow us to reach roughly three times as many people each week. We prayed about it, had peace, and moved forward with the loan.

Our rapid congregational growth continued in the new facility, and God opened up doors of opportunity to add more campuses. Accommodating this growth and seizing those opportunities required adding to our debt. Each time, we had peace to move forward, and each time, we were able to reach many more people—all the while keeping our debt service under our target level of 5 percent of our total budget. I'm hesitant to share the numbers with you, but please remember our church is a very large church. In this season of hypergrowth, our debt grew to over $60 million, but at the same time, our annual income grew to $140 million. That would be comparable to having $140,000 in income and a mortgage balance of $60,000.

Then a few years ago, we sensed the Spirit of God prompting us to become aggressive about paying off our debt. We, as a church body, did exactly what I've encouraged you to do as a household. We committed to a new budget structure that would pay off all our debt in five years.

After two years of following this budget, we had reduced the debt to $52 million. But we sensed we weren't being aggressive enough in attacking that balance. So, after doing some soul searching, we decided to reevaluate everything we were doing as an organization to make sure that we were helping people as effectively and as *efficiently* as possible. Just as with an individual household working to retire debt, this required making some difficult choices. Nevertheless, we made the necessary cutbacks and began applying the savings to our debt. As I have said before in previous chapters, the main truth I want you to catch from this book is that God supernaturally aids and blesses good stewards in the same way He does generous givers. The key—first, last, and always—is to obey what He's telling you.

> God supernaturally aids and blesses good stewards in the same way He does generous givers.

I'm pleased to tell you that God began to supernaturally bless us, and in just a few months, we paid off *all* our debt! That's right—$52 million in debt was retired supernaturally fast! My point is that if God can pay off $52 million in just a few short months, He can supernaturally bless you as well. What we anticipated taking five years God did in only three years, with the majority of the progress happening in the final four months!

Yes, there is a place and a time to borrow. But debt is a dangerous tool. Use it sparingly, prudently, and prayerfully. And make it your goal to be completely and utterly debt-free.

CHAPTER FIFTEEN

BLESSED TO BE A BLESSING

Mitch can still vividly remember what it felt like to be buried in debt and always under the gun financially. If he pauses to think about it, he can recall the stress, the fear, and the ever-present knot in his stomach. Even though it's been more than twelve years since he and his wife, Mandy, stepped onto the pathway that led them to a life beyond blessed, he can still put himself back into that horrible box in his imagination. He can clearly remember the wall of frustration they'd hit each time they saw someone in need or a ministry cause that touched their hearts and they were powerless to act meaningfully on their sincere desire to help.

"I didn't have a clue about what I was doing financially," Mitch recalls. "I was a knucklehead as it related to our money and up to my eyeballs in debt. And then everything changed." He will also tell you that he was very much immersed in Mammon's lie that he could achieve happiness if only he could accumulate enough "stuff."

What changed was his heart. As this couple regularly sat under my teaching about the principles of stewardship at Gateway Church,

God used two key Scriptures to convict and draw them onto that path. The first of these was Psalm 24:1:

> The earth is the Lord's, and all its fullness,
> the world and those who dwell therein.

Mitch began by wholeheartedly embracing one of the very first truths I presented in this book—namely, that all wise stewardship is built upon the foundational understanding that God owns it all, and that we are only temporary caretakers of what He has placed in our hands. That's what a "steward" is—someone who manages the property of the true owner. As long as we have an "owner" mind-set, we will never truly think like a steward.

> We are only temporary caretakers of what He has placed in our hands.

The second verse that turned Mitch around was 1 Corinthians 4:2:

> Moreover it is required in stewards that one be found faithful.

In other words, we really are all stewards, whether we recognize it or not. The only question is, Are you a good one or a bad one? What this verse revealed to Mitch is that the quality of our stewardship is measured in terms of "faithfulness." Mitch and Mandy determined they were going to become *faithful* stewards of what God had entrusted to them. Mitch says, "We accepted the challenge to start paying attention to our finances and to start living that out in a daily way."

They began by doing what I have advised you to do—by getting serious about crafting and living on a budget. Mitch confesses, with a laugh, that up to that point in his life, he would have rather passed a kidney stone than think about a budget. But he and Mandy acquired some budgeting resources and tools from Dave Ramsey's organization, rolled up their sleeves, and got to work. Going through that process together yielded benefits Mitch hadn't anticipated. "Through building our budget and sticking to it, Mandy and I learned how to be on the same page. A level of unity came into our marriage that we had never experienced before," he recalls. The couple quickly began to see results in other areas, too. "We paid off over $38,500 in debt in just fifteen months. Other than our mortgage note, we've been debt-free ever since." With their debt out of the way, they were able to build up an emergency fund that could accommodate almost any unforeseen contingency. As a result, all the stress, worry, fear, and pressure that had been a constant element of their life and relationship for the first ten years or so of their marriage suddenly evaporated.

If you were to sit down and talk to Mitch and Mandy, you might be surprised to learn that as wonderful as all that peace and freedom have been, they're not the best parts of their lives as faithful stewards.

Mitch says, "We have been tithing throughout this whole process. But as we got our financial lives in order, we began looking for places to give over and above our tithe. Today we give around twenty-five percent of our income to ministry—the tithe to our church and another fifteen percent to ministries God has given us a desire to help. On top of that, we have what we call our 'walking around blessing money.'" He's referring to the cash he and Mandy both carry for the express purpose of listening for the Spirit of God to speak to them about giving it away as they move through their daily lives.

"That's been phenomenally fun," Mitch says. "We are having an amazing time."

Your Pathway to "Happy" and Beyond

What Mitch and Mandy discovered is true. Giving is fun. You could say that sentence represents a three-word synopsis of my first book, *The Blessed Life*. As I've already stated several times, the most fun a human being can have this side of heaven comes when you have both the heart and the ability to be a miraculous expression of God's love to another person. Most people who love God have the heart to bless others financially, but only faithful stewards consistently have the ability to do so.

Helping you get to the place where you have that ability is precisely why I wrote this book. I want you to experience that kind of life. As I noted at the outset of this journey, the Greek word translated as "blessed" in our New Testament literally means "happy." And so a life beyond blessed implies there is something beyond happiness. And there is. What's better than happiness? Joy.

The life of a faithful steward is a joyful life. In chapter 1 I painted a picture of that life for you. I asked you to imagine always having money left at the end of the month, rather than too much month left at the end of your money. I invited you to picture a life in which you've forgotten what it feels like to have worry or stress about your finances. Imagine a life of daily peace, laying your head on your pillow at night with a satisfied soul, and sleeping like a baby. Envision a life of harmony, unity, peace, and purpose in your home, where, if you're married, you and your spouse routinely pray about spending priorities but never fight about money. I asked you to visualize not getting a sudden pit in your stomach when you think about your retirement years or old age, but rather, like the wise, prudent woman of Proverbs 31, you "smile at the future."

What I asked you to imagine was the life of a faithful steward. Because God blesses faithful stewards, it's literally a "blessed life"—that is, a happy life. But there is more. As wonderful as that happy life is, good stewardship isn't the end goal; it's the means to an end. The

---
Live a lifestyle of generosity.
---

real goal is what faithful stewardship makes possible—the adventure of a life as I described it in my first book. I'm talking about living a lifestyle of generosity.

That's why I also opened this book by asking you to picture a life in which you get to bless others whenever and wherever the Spirit moves you. I described a life turbocharged with excitement, purpose, and fulfillment because you get to consistently invest in the people and causes that mean the most to you.

Indeed, you spend your days looking for opportunities to be an answer to some desperate person's whispered prayer—routinely having the privilege of serving as a living, breathing, tangible manifestation of God's love for them. How fun this life is! However, joy here and now isn't the only benefit of this kind of life. This is a life that lays up treasure in heaven. The knowledge of this adds to your daily joy. ·

Happiness is great, but deep joy is even better. Yes, you're happy when you're blessed. But you step into joy when you bless others. You're happy when you understand that God has forgiven you your sins and you have a clean conscience. But joy is sharing Jesus with someone else and being a part of that person's experience of the very same miracle of cleansing. That's also what you experience when, because you've done what was necessary to live well within your means, you're able to financially support your church and other organizations that are introducing others to Jesus. By the way, this is precisely what Jesus had in mind when He cryptically exhorted His followers to use "unrighteous mammon" to "make friends" in Luke 16:

And I say to you, make friends for yourselves by unrighteous mammon, that when you fail, they may receive you into an everlasting home. He who *is* faithful in *what is* least is faithful also in much; and he who is unjust in *what is* least is unjust also in much. Therefore if you have not been faithful in the unrighteous mammon, who will commit to your trust the true *riches*? And if you have not been faithful in what is another man's, who will give you what is your own?

No servant can serve two masters; for either he will hate the one and love the other, or else he will be loyal to the one and despise the other. You cannot serve God and mammon. (Luke 16:9–13, emphasis added)

Jesus is saying when you use your money (unrighteous mammon) to help people hear and receive the gospel, you're literally making friends you probably won't meet until you "fail" (die) and go to heaven. Indeed, these friends are part of the "treasure" you're laying up there. As a faithful steward who has used his or her money this way, you'll arrive in heaven one day to an amazing greeting. A big part of that welcome will be people who want to hug you and

> I want you to experience the happiness and joy that come from being a faithful steward—both in this life and in the life to come.

thank you for being responsible for having delivered the truth about Jesus to them. These new friends will be some of the cherished and precious things to you when your life is over, and you step into eternity. There, you will say, "I only thought I knew what joy was."

For all the reasons I've cited, I hope you've taken the truths in this book to heart. I want you to experience the happiness and joy that come from being a faithful steward—both in this life and in the life to come.

God Is Looking for Faithful Stewards

Stewardship is your pathway to that happy life. You can't get there any other way. God speaks to me prophetically very frequently, so allow me to prophesy to you...I'm telling you again, you're not going to win the lottery. And even if you did, the sudden wealth would destroy you if you haven't learned to faithfully steward what God has placed in your hands. It is God's love for you that restrains Him from blessing you if you're a bad steward. As Jesus said in that passage about "unrighteous mammon,"

Whoever can be trusted with very little can also be trusted with much, and whoever is dishonest with very little will also be dishonest with much. (Luke 16:10 niv)

Even so, it's our heavenly Father's nature to bless. That's why He sincerely, fervently wants you to be "blessable." Allow me to say it again: God's principles of stewardship are for our sakes, not His. He's rooting for you to become a better steward because He's looking for people into whose hands He can put significant resources.

His eyes are scanning to and fro throughout the earth for faithful stewards willing to hold the wealth He gives them with an open, generous hand—people He can trust to give when His Spirit prompts them to give.

In the words of the old cliché, God will get it *to* you if He knows He can get it *through* you. When I think about this truth, I'm reminded of a wildly successful inventor friend of mine. This man has come up with several patented innovations related to the plumbing industry. Indeed, you probably have one or more of his products in or around your house. These have obviously made him an extremely wealthy individual. But he wasn't always well-off. He credits God with giving him his creative breakthroughs. However, if you ask him *why* he thinks God has blessed Him with these ideas, he'll tell you this story.

Years ago, he was a churchgoing believer with a modest income living in a modest house in a modest neighborhood. As it happened, that neighborhood was near the flight path for takeoffs and landings at Dallas / Fort Worth International Airport—one of the busiest air transportation hubs in the world.

At the time, his church was just launching a new building program and asking members to prayerfully make three-year giving commitments, over and above their regular giving, in support of the effort. So, one evening he was standing in his backyard praying and fellowshipping with God as commercial jets flew over his head. In the intimacy of that moment, he asked God how much He wanted him to pledge in total for the three-year campaign.

In response he clearly heard the Lord's inward voice in his spirit say, "I want you to give $50,000."

My friend will tell you that he literally laughed out loud and said, "Are You serious?" That amount represented an enormous sum of money for him and his wife to give, even when broken down into thirty-six monthly increments. Yet once again he heard the Lord's voice say, "Yes. I'm serious."

So, he stood there staring at the sky for a while, pondering what God had just asked him to do. My friend is a man of faith and a man with a heart to obey God, so he said, sort of to himself, "Well, God must be about to do something remarkable for us to be able to give that much. I guess the money is just going to sort of appear or something. It will be some sort of miracle if we're going to look back three years from now and have given $50,000."

About that time, while he was still looking at the sky, the voice of the Lord interrupted him and said, "Do you think I'm just going to drop that money out of the sky? What are you doing standing here looking up in the air? Go sit down at your computer and figure out how you're going to adjust your budget."

He laughed again and said, "You're right, Father. You've asked us to give this amount, so I guess I'd better go budget for it."

With his personal finance program open, he began looking at ways to cut and slash to enable them to start giving an additional $1,389 each month to the church. It literally seemed impossible at first. The money just wasn't there. He vividly recalls that at one point, he pointed to a group of line items in his budget that most people consider essentials, and said, "Father, the only way I can do what You've asked me to do is to take *these things* out of my budget." He assumed at that point God would say something like, "Oh my, you're right. I've made a math mistake. You can't give that much!" But that's not what he heard the Lord say in response.

The Lord said, "Okay!"

"Really, Lord? Is this really You?"

"Yes."

So he did it. He swallowed hard and made the cuts. However,

those cuts didn't have to stay in place for long. As soon as it was clear that he was serious about obeying, his business began to prosper and grow at a new level. Throughout the three-year span, he was able to fully fulfill the pledge that had seemed utterly impossible the night he made it. But that's not the end of the story.

On the final Sunday of the building campaign, he and his wife gave their thirty-sixth and final gift of $1,389 to the building fund. It was a wonderful feeling. The next evening, while still basking in the afterglow of that accomplishment, they heard a knock at their door. It was a representative of DFW Airport. As it turned out, the airport's governing authority had been ordered by a judge to compensate homeowners whose property values may have been negatively affected by increased traffic and noise from the ever-growing airport. This man was there to inform him that his house had fallen just inside the line drawn by a professional survey of affected homes. His next-door neighbor's house wasn't inside the line. But his was. Would you like to guess the amount of that compensation?

"We'll be sending you a check for $50,000," the man told him.

After picking his jaw up off the floor, my friend walked back out into his backyard to talk to God and watch airplanes fly over. In that moment he heard God's familiar voice once again.

"By the way, son, I can drop it out of the sky if I want to."

It was after this that my friend received his first million-dollar idea. He believes with all his heart that God gave him that idea and those that followed because He'd learned He could trust him with money. He'd been faithful and obedient with little, so God entrusted him with much more. He was faithful with that increase. So, even more increase came his way. Of course, this man remains one of the most obedient and generous givers to people and to the gospel I know. If God tells him to do something, he does it.

It's Your Turn

How will your stewardship story read? Where will your adventure take you? Naturally, I have no way of knowing. What I do know is that if you'll step out in faith and obedience—if you'll embrace the biblical truths that I've presented on these pages—God's power and supernatural enablement will rush in, in response to your sincere desire to be a faithful steward. Ask Him—He'll help you. He'll guide you.

As I told you early in this journey, walking down Stewardship Road is simple. I told you that stewardship, boiled down to its purest essence, just means doing these four life-giving things:

- I put God first in everything because He loves me and redeemed me (tithe/firstfruits).
- I gratefully receive everything God puts in my hand (be thankful).
- I steward faithfully what He has entrusted to me (budget).
- I hold His blessings with an open hand, prepared to give or distribute them as He directs, never forgetting that they are His, and that I am His (give).

Also, as I said at the outset, a life of true blessing walks on two legs. As we've seen, the vital first leg is learning to manage your financial resources so you can live within your means. This makes the second leg possible—living a lifestyle of generosity. It's a life in which you are generous toward God, toward your family, and toward others (in that

> God is a giver and you're never more like your heavenly Father than when you give.

order). It's a life in which you give for the sheer joy of giving, rather than expecting something in return. God is a giver and you're never more like your heavenly Father than when you give.

I want to close by reminding you of one additional blessing that results from living a life of wise stewardship. It's a huge one. I'm talking about the impact your life will have on the next generation and beyond. In an earlier chapter I pointed out that a life of stewardship and generosity will have a lasting impact on those around you, especially those most influenced by your example. As I mentioned, it's not really what we say that our children note and remember. It's what we model.

That truth came home to me in a major way one day with my own daughter a few years ago after I preached a sermon about generosity.

In that message, to illustrate a point, I shared a story about an unnamed man in our church who'd developed a practice of carrying $100 bills in his wallet at all times. This cash enabled him to bless others he encountered during his day as the Lord prompted him. That "man in our church" was actually me, but I didn't say so because I didn't want to draw attention to myself. I wasn't lying, because I am "a man" and I am "in our church"!

The specific story I shared with our congregation that day involved a struggling single mom in our church. After hearing me preach about putting God first through the tithe, she decided she was going to start tithing, even though her financial circumstances made it seem impossible to do so. The following Sunday, she brought her checkbook to church, and when it came time to write her tithe check—which was exactly $100—she felt a prompting from the Lord to write it out for $120 instead. She thought, "Lord, $100 is a huge stretch for me and now You're asking me to give more?" But in spite of her concern, she continued to sense that still, small voice and peace in her spirit. So, in faith and obedience, she wrote the check for $120 and dropped it in the offering box. As she was heading to her car after the service, the Lord pointed her out to *that* man in our church who gives $100 bills to people when the Lord tells him. He stopped her with the intention of giving her one of those bills, but when he reached in his wallet, he noticed a $20 bill right beside it and felt the Spirit of God prompting him to give her $120! And he did so.

Of course, she then shared with him she had just moments earlier taken that step of faith in tithing and had given over and above the tithe.

That is the story I shared in that sermon, without revealing that I was *that* man.

As it happened, we were having our adult children over for lunch that day. In the course of the visit, my daughter Elaine asked me if she could talk with me for a moment, so we stepped into another room. To comprehend the power of what she told me, you need to understand that although today my daughter is a powerful woman of God who has spoken to thousands in women's conferences, as a teenager there was a brief season when she walked away from the Lord. When she asked me if she could talk with me that afternoon, it was only a few years after she recommitted her life to Christ.

In that private moment, she looked deeply into my eyes and said, "Daddy, you're that man, aren't you?"

A little confused, I said, "What man, sweetie?"

"The man who gives away the $100 bills!"

I tried to be coy, and said, "Why do you think that?"

"Because today when you were sharing that story, I was suddenly flooded with memories from my childhood...memories of seeing you giving money to waitresses, sanitation workers, homeless people, single mothers, and on and on! I remember you doing that all the time as I was growing up. I guess I always just assumed you were giving them a few dollars. But they were $100 bills, weren't they?"

I confessed. "Yes, sugar, I am the man who gives people $100 bills when the Lord prompts me."

Her eyes swelled with tears and she said, "I want to be just like you, Daddy!"

With immense gratitude I can tell you honestly that not only does she love God with all her heart, she is one of the most generous people I know. But it's not because she's like me. It's because she is like her heavenly Father. Yet God used the example of what He was doing in and through me to inspire her. Now she and her wonderful husband are modeling stewardship and generosity for their children. And the blessing continues.

You see, wise stewardship impacts past, present, and future. It helps heal financial mistakes of the past, brings you peace in the present, and powerfully impacts the future. Your wise stewardship creates a lasting legacy that extends far beyond your brief time on this earth. It's that powerful.

> Stewardship impacts past, present, and future.

I'm excited for you. Get going! There is a happy journey to undertake, and great, great joy waiting for you as you live beyond blessed.

ACKNOWLEDGMENTS

I want to thank my son James for helping me write this book. Several years ago, he gave up his lifelong dream of owning his own business and joined me in ministry to help people understand these principles and truly live a life beyond blessed!

I also want to thank my friend and writing partner in several books, including this one, David Holland. You are truly a gift to the body of Christ, and I sincerely thank you for helping me help others for nearly two decades now!

NOTES

Chapter 1

1. Melissa Chan, "Here's How Winning the Lottery Makes You Miserable," *Time*, January 12, 2016, http://time.com/4176128/powerball-jackpot-lottery-winners/.

2. Ibid.

3. Robert Pagliarini, "Why Lottery Winners Crash After a Big Win," *Forbes*, September 27, 2013, https://www.forbes.com/sites/robertpagliarini/2013/09/27/why-lottery-winners-crash-after-a-big-win/#73b0dfce213c.

4. Ibid.

5. R. J. Tunney, *The Effects of Winning the Lottery on Happiness, Life, Satisfaction, and Mood* (United Kingdom: University of Nottingham, 2006).

6. American Psychological Association, "American Psychological Association Survey Shows Money Stress Weighing on Americans' Health Nationwide," February 4, 2015, https://www.apa.org/news/press/releases/2015/02/money-stress.aspx.

7. Angela Johnson, "76% of Americans Are Living Paycheck-to-Paycheck," CNN Money website, June 24, 2013, https://money.cnn.com/2013/06/24/pf/emergency-savings/index.html.

Chapter 3

1. *Francis of Assisi—the Saint: Early Documents*, ed. Regis J. Armstrong, vol. 1 (London: New City Press, 1999), 529, 534.

2. Kirsi I. Stjerna and Brooks Schramm, eds., *Encounters with Luther: New Direction for Critical Studies* (Louisville: Westminster John Knox Press, 2016), 223.

3. William Garden Blaikie, *The Life of David Livingstone: Chiefly from His Unpublished Journals and Correspondence in the Possession of His Family*, (London: J. Murray, 1903), 116.

Chapter 7

1. Brandon Gaille, "19 Dramatic Impulse Buying Statistics," BrandonGaille .com, May 22, 2017, https://brandongaille.com/18-dramatic-impulse-buying -statistics/.

Chapter 8

1. Mitchell Zuckoff, *Ponzi's Scheme: The True Story of a Financial Legend*, (New York: Random House, 2005), 15.
2. Crystal Lombardo, "The Impulse Shopping Fact Sheet," BetaBait.com, December 22, 2103, http://betabait.com/the-impulse-shopping-fact-sheet/.
3. Aimee Picchi, "The American Habit of Impulse Buying," Moneywatch, CBS News, January 25, 2016, https://www.cbsnews.com/news/the-american -habit-of-impulse-buying/.
4. Aimee Picchi, "Most Americans Can't Handle a $500 Surprise Bill," Moneywatch, CBS News, January 6, 2016, https://www.cbsnews.com/news /most-americans-cant-handle-a-500-surprise-bill/.
5. Kay Bell, "Tax Refund Loans, Checks Still Cost Taxpayers Lots of Money," Don't Mess with Taxes website, April 9, 2018, http://www.dontmesswith taxes.com/2018/04/tax-refund-loans-and-advance-checks-still-costing -taxpayers-too-much-money-says-consumer-report.html.
6. Michael Corkery and Stacy Crowley, "Household Debt Makes a Comeback in the U.S.," *The New York Times*, May 17, 2017, https://www.nytimes .com/2017/05/17/business/dealbook/household-debt-united-states.html.
7. Caitlin Dewey, "A Stunning Map of Depression Rates Around the World," *The Washington Post*, November 7, 2013, https://www.washingtonpost.com/news /worldviews/wp/2013/11/07/a-stunning-map-of-depression-rates-around-the -world.
8. Student Loan Hero, "A Look at the Shocking Student Loan Debt Statistics for 2018," May 1, 2018, https://studentloanhero.com/student-loan-debt-statistics/.
9. Ibid.
10. Ibid.

11. Richard Fry, "For First Time in Modern Era, Living with Parents Edges Out Other Living Arrangements for 18- to 34-Year-Olds," Pew Research Center, May 24, 2016, http://www.pewsocialtrends.org/2016/05/24/for-first-time-in-modern-era-living-with-parents-edges-out-other-living-arrangements-for-18-to-34-year-olds/.

Chapter 9

1. Thayer and Smith. Greek Lexicon entry for Egkataleipo, "The KJV New Testament Greek Lexicon"

Chapter 11

1. "Goals Research Summary," Dominican University, https://www.dominican.edu/academics/lae/undergraduate-programs/psych/faculty/assets-gail-matthews/researchsummary2.pdf.

2. Ibid.

3. Ibid.

4. Rick Warren, "9 Actions You Must Take to Reach Your Biggest Goals (Part 1)," pastors.com, January 2, 2015, http://pastors.com/big-goals-1/.

5. Jack Canfield, *The Success Principles: How to Get from Where You Are to Where You Want to Be* (New York: Collins, 2005), 51.

6. Zig Ziglar, *See You at the Top* (New Orleans: Pelican Publishing, 1977), 168.

Chapter 12

1. Robert Morris, *The Blessed Life* (Southlake, Texas: Gateway Publishing, 2016), 140–141.

Chapter 13

1. Stephen Covey, A. Roger Merrill, and Rebecca Merrill, *First Things First* (New York: Free Press, 1994), 88.

Chapter 14

1. Maria Lamagna, "Americans Now Have the Highest Credit-Card Debt in U.S. History," MarketWatch, August 8, 2017, https://www.marketwatch.com/story/us-households-will-soon-have-as-much-debt-as-they-had-in-2008-2017-04-03.

ABOUT THE AUTHOR

ROBERT MORRIS is the founding lead senior pastor of Gateway Church, a multicampus church based out of the Dallas–Fort Worth metroplex. Since it began in 2000, the church has grown to more than 71,000 active attendees. His television program is aired in over 190 countries, and his radio program, *Worship & the Word with Pastor Robert*, airs in more than 1,800 radio markets across America. He serves as chancellor of The King's University and is the bestselling author of numerous books, including *The Blessed Life*, *Frequency*, *Beyond Blessed*, and *Take the Day Off*. Robert and his wife, Debbie, have been married thirty-nine years and are blessed with one married daughter, two married sons, and nine grandchildren.